Simply
Australian
Barbecue Recipes

Catherine Atkinson

foulsham
LONDON • NEW YORK • TORONTO • SYDNEY

foulsham

The Publishing House, Bennetts Close,
Cippenham, Slough, Berkshire, SL1 5AP, England

ISBN 0-572-02581-5

Cover photograph © Struan Wallace

Printed in Great Britain by Cox & Wyman Ltd., Reading, Berks

CONTENTS

INTRODUCTION

Australia does get cloudy skies and rain, but more often the days are filled with endless sunshine. Alongside this great climate is an abundance of fresh fruit and vegetables, a plentiful supply of free-range meat and, in the warm seas that surround the country, a huge range of seafood and exotic fish. It's no wonder that the barbecue epitomises Australian cooking!

Every Australian home, hotel and picnic spot has a barbecue, often just a converted oil drum with a metal sheet on top instead of a grid. In city parks you'll find barbecue areas with electric hotplates – bring your food along, put money in the slot and you can start cooking.

People of different nationalities from all over the globe have settled in Australia. British settlers were the first, over 200 years ago, but in the last 50 years many new arrivals from other parts of Europe and Asia have influenced the cuisine, the largest numbers coming from Greece, Italy, Vietnam, Thailand and China.

The recipes here will fire your imagination and suit every barbecue occasion, whether it's a party, family get-together or just a simple evening or midday meal. Clear step-by-step instructions make barbecuing easy, leaving you more time to spend in the great outdoors.

BARBECUE BASICS

In essence, a barbecue is simply burning coals with a grate suspended over them to hold the food, but the huge range available, some very sophisticated, can be daunting. Buy a barbecue that matches your needs; you can spend as little or as much as you like, although it's not worth investing in an expensive model if you only use it once a year. Check out the cooking space on the rack, especially if you plan to cook for large numbers and make sure that you have enough storage space to put the whole thing away when the barbecue season comes to an end.

The **'hibachi'** – the Japanese word for 'firebowl' is one of the most popular and simplest portable barbecues. A grate holds the charcoal just above the base, so that air can circulate beneath through vents and the food is cooked on a rack set above. On the largest version, enough food can be cooked for 10–12 people.

Covered kettles are free-standing, round barbecues which come in several sizes. The rounded metal lid reflects heat all over the cooking area, so the food cooks evenly. They're particularly good for cooking larger joints of meat and whole birds.

Set on a rectangular portable trolley, **hooded barbecues** are similar to covered kettles in that they can be used covered or open. Dampers, which regulate air flow, and movable grills allow you to control the heat and they often come with extras such as warming racks and rotisseries.

At the cheapest end of the market are **disposable barbecues** – ready-to-use trays already filled with charcoal and firelighter. Simply set fire to the tray and wait about 20 minutes for it to get hot. They're perfect for barbecue picnics and places where space is limited, such as patios or even roof gardens!

With most barbecues, food is cooked over charcoal. In a gas or electric barbecue, lava rock is heated by an electric element or gas flame. The temperature is easy to control and the barbecue only takes 10 minutes to heat up ready for cooking, compared to a standard barbecue that takes about 40 minutes. The special barbecue flavour comes from the aromatic smoke which is made when fats and juices in the food drip on to the coals – whether charcoal or lava rock.

Aussie Lingo

Aussie	Australian
barbie	barbecue
bug	a small crab
billy	can for boiling water in
chook	chicken
cut lunch	sandwiches
dog's eye	meat pie
esky	cool box
fish 'n' greasies	fish and chips
flake	shark
hot bread shop	bakery
jaffle	toasted sandwich
lollies	sweets
pav	pavlova (a meringue dessert with cream and fruit)
savouries	canapés/finger food
slices	cakes
snags, snaggers or mystery bags	sausages
spicy tucker	ethnic food
yabbies	crayfish

Equipment

The key to barbecue cooking is simplicity, so, to make sure everything runs smoothly, gather all the necessary equipment to hand before you begin.

For the Fire

* Charcoal or briquettes, firelighters, tapers, matches.
* Heavy-duty foil to line the barbecue (to make it easier to clean afterwards).
* Tongs for moving the hot coals.
* Spray bottle filled with water in case of flare-ups.
* Bucket of water, just in case.
* A wire brush to scrub the barbecue rack and a specialist barbecue cleaner for cleaning up afterwards.

For the Food and Cooking

* Thick oven gloves are a must; make sure they're heat-resistant. A large apron is useful.
* Use long-handled tongs for turning food as it cooks. Check that they meet in the middle to hold food securely and go for a pair with wooden handles as metal can become very hot and plastic may melt.
* Keep a fork handy for spearing food to check it's done.
* A long-handled basting brush is useful for applying oil and bastes during cooking. Buy one designed for barbecuing or use a paintbrush (for food use only!).
* Choose long, flat, sturdy skewers for heavy foods. Bamboo and wooden skewers can be used for light quick-cooking foods, but must be soaked in water for about 30 minutes first, to reduce the chance of them charring on the barbecue.

* Hinged wire baskets are an asset when cooking whole fish and other delicate items which might otherwise break when being turned. Brush the basket with oil first to stop the food from sticking.
* A meat thermometer is a foolproof way of cooking joints of meat or whole birds as you won't have to keep piercing the meat to check if it's done.
* Have a small table or trolley near the barbecue for equipment, uncooked foods, bastes, serving plates and garnishes.

For Serving

* Ideally, have a large table to eat at, as you'll need plenty of room for accompaniments. Alternatively, set out a separate table for these.
* On a hot day, put up an umbrella or awning for shade.
* Set out crockery and cutlery, including serving spoons, napkins and a tray of condiments.
* Have ready plenty of glasses, cold drinks, jugs of water and ice and icepacks in a coolbox. Encourage everyone to help themselves, so that you can relax and enjoy the barbecue as well.

Barbecue Watch Points

* Always let your neighbours know that you're planning to have a barbecue.
* Avoid accidents by setting the barbecue on a level surface, away from the house and overhanging trees or shrubs. Don't use petrol or lighter fuel to light the barbecue, and douse the fire when you've finished cooking.
* Keep children and pets well away from the barbecue and never touch it once lit – and remember, very hot charcoal looks white and powdery, not glowing red.

If you do get burned, immerse the injury in cold water until it no longer stings. Cover with a dry, sterile dressing, if necessary, and seek medical attention if severe.

✳ Keep your eye on the barbecue at all times; this is vital for safety reasons and should a flare-up occur, you'll be able to rescue the food before it gets burnt.

✳ Keep food chilled and covered until you are ready to cook.

✳ Check that food is cooked through before serving. If the heat is too high the outside may char, while the inside is still raw. Don't overcrowd the rack by cooking everything at once. Space allows the heat to penetrate more efficiently.

Lighting and Maintaining the Fire

✳ Line the barbecue with heavy-duty foil, shiny side up, and open the vents if your barbecue has them.

✳ Break a few firelighters and scatter over the foil. Alternatively, use a few sheets of newspaper, rolled up tightly into tubes.

✳ Add a few pieces of lump charcoal (these burn hotter than briquettes and are ideal for quick cooking at the beginning of the barbecue when everyone's hungry and waiting), then arrange some briquettes on top.

✳ Light the firelighters or newspaper with a taper. As the fire grows, add more coals. When the coals are hot, spread them out, using tongs.

✳ Most charcoal burns for 45 minutes to 1 hour, so for longer cooking times you'll need to add more charcoal. Add just a few at a time, using long-handled tongs.

✳ If you have a lot of charcoal left at the end of the cooking time, douse with sand and leave until cold to save and use for your next barbecue.

Starting to Cook

* The fire should take 30–40 minutes to reach cooking temperature. When the coals begin to form a light layer of white ash and you can hold your hand no closer than 15 cm/6 in from the coals for about 3 seconds, the fire is ready.

* The centre of the fire is always the hottest, so this is the place to sear meat such as steak, before moving to a cooler part to cook through.

* Plan your cooking, so you start with foods that will take the longest time to cook.

* Larger pieces of meat, such as chicken legs and rack of lamb, improve by 'resting' on the warming rack, or the coolest part of the barbecue, for about 10 minutes before serving.

* If you're catering for large numbers, get a head start by precooking some of the food, such as chicken portions, which can then be simply finished on the barbecue. Give baked potatoes up to an hour in the oven before bringing them out to finish off on the coals.

* Put sauces and breads to warm at the edge of the barbecue, while cooking the rest of the food.

* Place desserts on the barbecue to cook while you eat your main course or wait until you've eaten – it's a good idea to leave a gap between courses.

BARBECUE STORECUPBOARD

If, like the Australians, you enjoy impromptu barbecues, it makes sense to keep a few basic ingredients in the storecupboard, fridge and freezer, so you're ready to barbie as soon as the sun comes out.

Listed below are the standby foods I find most useful – customise the list to include your own favourites.

In the Cupboard

* Dried spices and seasonings – cumin seeds and powder; ground coriander (cilantro), turmeric, chilli, ginger and paprika; grated nutmeg; whole cloves, peppercorns and star anise for marinades and dry spice rubs. Store them in a cool dark place and buy in small quantities as they soon lose their pungency. You will also need garlic, chillis and ginger, either fresh or minced in bottles or tubes.

* Dried herbs – bay leaves, oregano, thyme, rosemary and mixed herbs. If possible, though, grow some fresh herbs in pots on the windowsill or in the garden.

* Sauces – tomato ketchup (catsup), tomato purée (paste), Worcestershire sauce, pesto, hoisin, light and dark soy sauce, English, wholegrain and Dijon mustards, and mayonnaise.

* Vinegars – red and white wine, cider, rice and fruit vinegars. In the recipes specific vinegars are called for, but you can usually substitute another type instead if necessary. It's worth buying a small bottle of balsamic vinegar, however: there is no substitute for its dark colour and smooth, mellow flavour. You can also flavour your own vinegars by adding a few sprigs of

fresh herbs such as thyme or rosemary or a couple of chillis, pricked with a fine skewer, then leaving to infuse for a week. Use them within two months.

* Oils – olive, either 'light' or 'extra-virgin', which is darker in colour with a strong fruity flavour; sunflower oil, or groundnut oil and sesame seed oil, which gives an intense nutty taste and frequently features in oriental recipes.

* Juices – lemon and lime, either as fruit or bottled.

* Cans or jars – creamed coconut, sun-dried tomatoes in oil, capers, fruit such as peaches and pineapple, and clear honey, preferably the dark-coloured, strongly flavoured Australian eucalyptus variety.

* Nuts and seeds, including macademias and sesame seeds; and peanut butter.

* Relishes and chutneys.

In the Freezer

* Lean minced (ground) meat – steak, lamb, chicken or turkey for burgers and meatballs.

* Lean meat or fish cuts – beef, lamb, salmon or tuna steaks and chicken breasts.

* A selection of different sausages.

* Whole fish – snapper, red mullet or barramundi.

* Shellfish – large raw prawns (shrimp) and other shellfish such as scallops and prepared squid (buy them ready-frozen or, if buying fresh, check that they haven't been previously frozen).

* Part-baked baguettes or ready-prepared garlic bread.

* Herbs such as parsley and coriander (cilantro), chopped and frozen ready for use.

* Good-quality flavoured ice creams, such as vanilla, coconut and toffee, to serve on their own or to accompany barbecued desserts.

BASIC COOKING TIMES

The table below is a basic guide to cooking on the barbecue. Remember that timings are only approximate and will vary according to the heat of the coals and the thickness of the food. Meat and fish should be marinated first, or brushed with a little oil and seasoning to keep them moist during cooking.

Food	Size	Cooking time on each side
BEEF		
Burgers	2.5 cm/1 in thick	3 minutes – rare
		5 minutes – medium
		6–8 minutes – well done
Steaks	2.5 cm/1 in thick	3–4 minutes – rare
		5–6 minutes – medium
		7 minutes – well done
Kebabs		5 minutes – medium
LAMB		
Cutlets	2 cm/¾ in thick	5–6 minutes
Chops or steaks	2.5 cm/1 in thick	4–5 minutes – rare
		6–7 minutes – medium
Lamburgers	2.5 cm/1 in thick	6 minutes
PORK		
Chops	2.5 cm/1 in thick	6–8 minutes
Kebabs		5–6 minutes
Sausages	thin	4–5 minutes
	thick	6–8 minutes
Ham/gammon steaks	1 cm/½ in thick	5 minutes

POULTRY

Chicken breasts, boned		8–10 minutes
Chicken portion with bone		15 minutes
Drumsticks		10–12 minutes
Wings		10 minutes
Turkey breast steaks	2 cm/¾ in thick	5 minutes
Duck breasts		10 minutes
Duck legs		15–20 minutes

FISH

Whole	large	10–15 minutes
	small	3–6 minutes
Steaks	2.5 cm/1 in thick	4–5 minutes
Kebabs		4–5 minutes
Prawns (shrimp)		3–5 minutes
Lobster		6 minutes

NOTES ON THE RECIPES

* When following a recipe, use either metric, imperial or American measures; do not mix different sets of measurements.

* All spoon measurements are level: 1 tsp = 5 ml;
  1 tbsp = 15 ml.

* All eggs are medium.

* The use of strongly flavoured ingredients such as garlic, chilli and ginger depends on personal taste and quantities can be adjusted accordingly.

* Always use fresh herbs unless dried ones are specifically called for. If you can't get fresh, try the chopped frozen varieties instead, or if using dried, use about a third of the quantity given for freshly chopped herbs.

* Always wash and peel, if necessary, all fresh produce before use.

* Preparation and cooking times are approximate. The time it takes for food to cook will depend on personal preference, the heat of the barbecue and how far from the coals you set the rack.

APPETISERS

There's nothing quite like the tantalising smell of food
cooked over hot coals to stimulate the appetite. With a
little thought beforehand, you can keep your diners
happy with these simple starters while they wait for the
main course. All of them can be prepared in advance
and are quick and easy to cook.
Keep appetisers small and light – they should just take
the edge off hunger and tantalise the taste buds for the
dishes still to come.

Mini Meatball Kebabs

The Greek community has strongly influenced Australian cuisine. Ingredients such as bulgar (cracked wheat), pine nuts and oregano feature in many recipes.

Serves 4

	METRIC	IMPERIAL	AMERICAN
Bulgar	50 g	2 oz	½ cup
Boiling vegetable or beef stock	250 ml	8 fl oz	1 cup
Minced (ground) beef	450 g	1 lb	1 lb
Finely chopped pine nuts	25 g	1 oz	¼ cup
Chopped fresh oregano	15 ml	1 tbsp	1 tbsp
Chopped fresh mint	15 ml	1 tbsp	1 tbsp
Egg yolk	1	1	1
Salt and freshly ground black pepper			
Small courgettes (zucchini)	2	2	2
Mint jelly	45 ml	3 tbsp	3 tbsp
Lemon juice	15 ml	1 tbsp	1 tbsp

1 Put the bulgar in a bowl and pour over the boiling stock. Leave to stand for 30 minutes, then drain well. When cool, squeeze out the excess liquid.

2 Mix together the bulgar, minced beef, pine nuts, herbs and egg yolk in a bowl, seasoning with salt and pepper. Shape the mixture into 2.5 cm/1 in balls.

3 Trim the courgettes and cut into 1 cm/½ in slices. Thread the meatballs and courgettes on to soaked wooden skewers.

4 Gently heat the mint jelly and lemon juice until melted. Carefully brush over the kebabs.

5 Barbecue the kebabs for about 10 minutes until well browned and cooked through, turning once or twice and brushing with the mint glaze.

 Preparation time: 10 minutes + 30 minutes standing
Cooking time: 10 minutes

Sticky Honey and Orange Chicken Wings

Barbecuing is an ideal way to cook chicken wings – succulent inside with crisp brown skins, they make a great starter.

Serves 4

	METRIC	IMPERIAL	AMERICAN
Chicken wings	16	16	16
Clear honey	30 ml	2 tbsp	2 tbsp
Finely grated orange rind	10 ml	2 tsp	2 tsp
Orange juice	30 ml	2 tbsp	2 tbsp
Tomato ketchup (catsup)	30 ml	2 tbsp	2 tbsp
Dark soy sauce	15 ml	1 tbsp	1 tbsp
Garlic clove, peeled and crushed	1	1	1
Freshly ground black pepper			
Chopped fresh coriander (cilantro) or parsley, to garnish	30 ml	2 tbsp	2 tbsp

1   Cut the tips off the chicken wings. Mix together the honey, orange rind and juice, tomato ketchup, soy sauce, garlic and pepper.

2   Thread the chicken wings on to four lightly greased metal skewers. Brush generously with the honey and orange mixture.

3   Barbecue for about 15 minutes, turning and basting several times during cooking, until crisp and browned.

4   Sprinkle the chicken wings with coriander or parsley and serve straight away.

Preparation time: 10 minutes
Cooking time: 15 minutes

Coriander and Chilli Mushrooms

This simple starter also makes an ideal vegetable accompaniment to barbecued steak. The flavour is fairly hot, so use just one chilli if you prefer.

Serves 4

	METRIC	IMPERIAL	AMERICAN
Butter, softened	75 g	3 oz	⅓ cup
Garlic clove, crushed	1	1	1
Red chilli, seeded and chopped	1	1	1
Green chilli, seeded and chopped	1	1	1
Chopped fresh coriander (cilantro)	45 ml	3 tbsp	3 tbsp
Salt and freshly ground black pepper			
Large flat mushrooms	450 g	1 lb	1 lb

1 Mix together the butter, garlic, chillis and coriander in a bowl, seasoning with salt and pepper.

2 Neatly trim the mushroom stalks with a sharp knife. Divide the butter between the mushrooms, spreading out with the back of the spoon.

3 Barbecue the mushrooms, stalk-side up, for about 10 minutes, or until very tender. Serve hot.

 Preparation time: 15 minutes
Cooking time: 10 minutes

Chargrilled Potato Wedges with Three Dips

Make the dips in advance and chill until ready to serve.

Serves 4

	METRIC	IMPERIAL	AMERICAN
Large baking potatoes, scrubbed	3	3	3
Sunflower oil	45 ml	3 tbsp	3 tbsp
Butter	25 g	1 oz	2 tbsp
Garlic clove, crushed	1	1	1
Salt and freshly ground black pepper			

1 Cut the potatoes into large thick wedges. Add to a large pan of boiling salted water and cook for 3 minutes. Drain in a colander, then tip into a bowl.

2 Melt the oil, butter, garlic, salt and pepper in a small pan. Drizzle over the potatoes, then gently toss to coat.

3 Barbecue the potato wedges for about 12 minutes, or until lightly browned and tender. Serve hot with the dips.

Preparation time: 10 minutes
Cooking time: 15 minutes

Blue Cheese and Onion Dip: 225 g/8 oz/2 cups crumbled blue cheese, 6 finely chopped spring onions (scallions), 120 ml/ 4 fl oz/½ cup soured (dairy sour) cream and black pepper.

Tuna and Tomato Dip: 185 g/6½ oz/1 small can drained and flaked tuna, 2 skinned, seeded and chopped tomatoes, 15 ml/ 1 tbsp drained capers, 175 ml/6 fl oz/¾ cup fromage frais, 5 ml/1 tsp tomato purée (paste), salt and black pepper.

Avocado Dip: Flesh of 1 avocado mashed with 15 ml/ 1 tbsp lemon or lime juice, 1 crushed garlic clove, 100 ml/3½ fl oz/scant ½ cup mayonnaise, 15 ml/1 tbsp snipped fresh chives, salt and pepper.

Smoky Bacon and Oyster Rolls with Caper Dip

Serves 4

	METRIC	IMPERIAL	AMERICAN
Can of smoked oysters	105 g	4 oz	1 small
Rashers (slices) of smoked streaky bacon	6	6	6
Tomato purée (paste)	5 ml	1 tsp	1 tsp
Red wine vinegar	10 ml	2 tsp	2 tsp
Light brown sugar	5 ml	1 tsp	1 tsp
Mustard powder	2.5 ml	½ tsp	½ tsp
Sunflower oil	10 ml	2 tsp	2 tsp
Mayonnaise	75 ml	5 tbsp	5 tbsp
Thick plain yoghurt	75 ml	5 tbsp	5 tbsp
Capers, drained and chopped	15 ml	1 tbsp	1 tbsp
Freshly ground black pepper			

1 Drain the oysters and pat dry on kitchen paper (paper towels). Stretch each rasher of bacon with the back of a knife and cut in half.

2 Mix together the tomato purée, vinegar, sugar, mustard powder and sunflower oil. Brush the mixture over the oysters.

3 Place an oyster at one end of each bacon rasher and roll up. Secure with a soaked wooden cocktail stick (toothpick).

4 For the Caper Dip, mix together the mayonnaise, yoghurt, capers and pepper. Chill until ready to serve.

5 Barbecue the bacon-wrapped oysters for about 5 minutes, until the bacon is crisp and browned, turning once. Serve straight away with the Caper Dip.

Preparation time: 15 minutes
Cooking time: 5 minutes

Crispy Tomato Crostini

The simplest way to skin tomatoes is to immerse them in boiling water for about 30 seconds, then plunge into cold water – the skins should then peel off easily.

Makes about 24

	METRIC	IMPERIAL	AMERICAN
Ripe plum tomatoes	2	2	2
Sun-dried tomato purée (paste)	15 ml	1 tbsp	1 tbsp
Olive oil	30 ml	2 tbsp	2 tbsp
Garlic clove, crushed	1	1	1
French stick	1	1	1

1 Skin the tomatoes, seed, then chop finely. Mix with the tomato purée, olive oil and garlic.

2 Cut the French stick into 2.5 cm/1 in diagonal slices. Spread one side with the tomato mixture.

3 Cook the tomato crostini on an oiled barbecue rack for about 2 minutes on each side until crisp. Serve hot.

Preparation time: 10 minutes
Cooking time: 4 minutes

Hot Crab-filled Avocado

Serves 4

	METRIC	IMPERIAL	AMERICAN
Large ripe avocados	2	2	2
Lemon juice	30 ml	2 tbsp	2 tbsp
Mayonnaise	90 ml	6 tbsp	6 tbsp
Dijon mustard	5 ml	1 tsp	1 tsp
Chopped fresh dill (dill weed)	30 ml	2 tbsp	2 tbsp
Anchovy fillets in oil, drained and finely chopped	4	4	4
Freshly ground black pepper			
Fresh or canned crabmeat	175 g	6 oz	6 oz
Sprigs of fresh dill, to garnish			

1 Cut the avocados in half lengthwise and remove the stones (pits). Brush the cut avocado all over with 15 ml/1 tbsp of the lemon juice.

2 Mix together the mayonnaise with the mustard, dill, anchovy fillets, the remaining lemon juice and the ground pepper. Gently mix in the crab, taking care not to break it up too much.

3 Pile the mixture into the avocados. Put each avocado half on a square of double-thickness kitchen foil.

4 Barbecue the avocados for about 8 minutes until warmed through. Serve garnished with sprigs of fresh dill.

Preparation time: 10 minutes
Cooking time: 8 minutes

Gingered King Prawns with Soured Cream Dip

Serves 4

	METRIC	IMPERIAL	AMERICAN
Raw king prawns (jumbo shrimp), peeled	450 g	1 lb	1 lb
Sunflower oil	15 ml	1 tbsp	1 tbsp
Piece of fresh root ginger, peeled and grated	5 cm	2 in	2 in
Garlic clove, crushed	1	1	1
Light soy sauce	15 ml	1 tbsp	1 tbsp
Lime juice	30 ml	2 tbsp	2 tbsp
Soured (dairy sour) cream	150 ml	¼ pint	⅔ cup
Capers, drained and chopped	15 ml	1 tbsp	1 tbsp
Chopped fresh dill (dill weed)	30 ml	2 tbsp	2 tbsp
Salt and freshly ground black pepper			

1 Cut along the underside of each prawn, taking care not to cut in half. Open out, flatten and remove the black thread.

2 Mix together the oil, ginger, garlic, soy sauce and lime juice in a bowl. Add the prawns, toss to coat, then cover and marinate in the fridge for 1 hour.

3 Mix together the soured cream, capers and dill, seasoning with salt and pepper. Cover and chill until ready to serve.

4 Put the prawns in a hinged basket if you have one or thread on to skewers. Barbecue for about 4 minutes until pink, turning once. Serve hot with the dip.

 Preparation time: 15 minutes + 1 hour marinating
Cooking time: 4 minutes

Devilled Squid Skewers

Don't marinate the squid for more than 30 minutes, or it will lose its firm texture.

Serves 4

	METRIC	IMPERIAL	AMERICAN
Large squid (calamari) hoods	450 g	1 lb	1 lb
Olive oil	30 ml	2 tbsp	2 tbsp
Lemon juice	15 ml	1 tbsp	1 tbsp
Light brown sugar	10 ml	2 tsp	2 tsp
Mustard powder	2.5 ml	½ tsp	½ tsp
Tabasco sauce	1.5 ml	¼ tsp	¼ tsp
Lemon wedges, to serve			

1   Cut the squid lengthwise into 1 cm/½ in strips. Mix together the oil, lemon juice, sugar, mustard powder and Tabasco sauce. Add the squid and toss to coat well. Cover and marinate in the fridge for 30 minutes.

2   Remove the squid from the marinade and thread in a 'concertina' fashion on to soaked wooden skewers.

3   Barbecue for 2–3 minutes on each side, until just opaque. Serve hot with wedges of lemon.

 Preparation time: 10 minutes + 30 minutes marinating
Cooking time: 5 minutes

BEEF

Think of barbecues and the aroma of a sizzling steak, crusty and mahogany brown on the outside, juicy and slightly pink within, comes to mind. The best cuts of beef for barbecuing are the prime cuts, such as fillet, sirloin and rump, which remain tender after quick cooking over direct heat. Choose steaks with a light marbling of fat which will keep them moist during cooking. Marinades will tenderise them further, as well as adding flavour and keeping the meat succulent. Before cooking, trim any excess fat from beef and other meats, so that it does not drip on to the coals, causing them to flare up. Test steaks to see if they are cooked by piercing with the tip of a knife (not too often or they will dry out). In a rare steak the juices will be red, for medium they will be slightly pink, and when well done, they'll run clear.

Beach Burgers

A combination of beef and pork is used for these burgers to give extra texture and flavour. Because they contain pork, it's important to cook them thoroughly.

Serves 4

	METRIC	IMPERIAL	AMERICAN
Lean minced (ground) beef	450 g	1 lb	1 lb
Lean minced pork	225 g	8 oz	8 oz
Fresh white breadcrumbs	25 g	1 oz	½ cup
Egg, beaten	1	1	1
Salt and freshly ground black pepper			
Sesame seed buns	4	4	4
Sliced tomatoes, shredded lettuce, onion rings, pickled gherkins (cornichons), mustard, mayonnaise and tomato ketchup (catsup), to serve			

1   Mix the minced beef and pork, breadcrumbs and egg together in a bowl, seasoning well with salt and pepper.

2   Divide the mixture into four and shape each portion into a burger about 2 cm/¾ in thick. Chill in the fridge for at least 1 hour if time allows.

3   Barbecue the burgers for about 5–6 minutes on each side until well browned on the outside and cooked through.

4   Meanwhile, split the sesame seed buns and toast for about 1 minute on the barbecue. Serve each burger in a bun with a choice of sauces and garnishes.

 Preparation time: 10 minutes + 1 hour chilling
Cooking time: 14 minutes

Mega Beef Burgers

To make the burgers easy to turn on the barbecue, cook them in a hinged wire basket if you have one.

Serves 4

	METRIC	IMPERIAL	AMERICAN
Minced (ground) steak	700g	1½ lb	1½ lb
Small onion, grated or very finely chopped	1	1	1
Garlic clove, crushed	1	1	1
Worcestershire sauce	30 ml	2 tbsp	2 tbsp
Made English mustard	2.5 ml	½ tsp	½ tsp
Chopped fresh parsley	30 ml	2 tbsp	2 tbsp
Egg, lightly beaten	1	1	1
Salt and freshly ground black pepper			
Rashers (slices) of smoked streaky bacon	4	4	4
Burger buns	4	4	4
Peach and Port Chutney (see page 138), salad leaves and mayonnaise, to serve			

1 Mix together the minced steak, onion, garlic, Worcestershire sauce, mustard, parsley and egg in a bowl, seasoning well with salt and pepper.

2 Shape the mixture into four burgers, cover and chill in the fridge for at least 1 hour.

3 Barbecue the burgers for about 7 minutes on each side, depending on thickness, until cooked through.

4 Meanwhile, cook the bacon on the barbecue for about 3 minutes on each side, until browned.

5 Serve the burgers in split buns, topped with the bacon, Peach and Port Chutney, salad leaves and mayonnaise, if liked.

Preparation time: 10 minutes + 1 hour chilling
Cooking time: 14 minutes

Surf and Turf

The name of these kebabs, which originated in Australia, refers to the prawns (shrimp) from the sea and the beef from the land.

Serves 4

	METRIC	IMPERIAL	AMERICAN
Rump or sirloin steak	*450 g*	*1 lb*	*1 lb*
Raw prawns	*16*	*16*	*16*
Oyster sauce	*60 ml*	*4 tbsp*	*4 tbsp*
Sunflower oil	*45 ml*	*3 tbsp*	*3 tbsp*
Soy sauce	*30 ml*	*2 tbsp*	*2 tbsp*
Lemon or lime juice	*30 ml*	*2 tbsp*	*2 tbsp*
Clear honey	*5 ml*	*1 tsp*	*1 tsp*
Salt and freshly ground black pepper			

1. Trim any fat from the steak, then cut into 2.5 cm/1 in cubes. Peel the prawns, leaving the tails attached.

2. To make the marinade, mix together the oyster sauce, oil, soy sauce, lemon or lime juice, honey, salt and pepper.

3. Add the steak and prawns to the marinade and toss together to coat completely. Cover and leave to marinate for 20 minutes.

4. Remove the steak and prawns, reserving the marinade for basting, and thread on to metal or soaked wooden skewers, alternating the steak with the prawns.

5. Barbecue the kebabs for about 8 minutes, turning occasionally and brushing with the remaining marinade during cooking, until the beef is browned and the prawns pink.

 Preparation time: 15 minutes + 20 minutes marinating
Cooking time: 8 minutes

Beer-basted Sirloin Steaks

Don't drizzle too much marinade at a time over the steaks during cooking, as the alcohol may make the fire flare up.

Serves 4

	METRIC	IMPERIAL	AMERICAN
Beef sirloin steaks, 2.5 cm/1 in thick	4	4	4
Brown ale or stout	100 ml	3½ fl oz	scant ½ cup
Dark Muscovado sugar	15 ml	1 tbsp	1 tbsp
Worcestershire sauce	15 ml	1 tbsp	1 tbsp
Sunflower oil	15 ml	1 tbsp	1 tbsp
Black or tropical peppercorns	10 ml	2 tsp	2 tsp
Fire-roasted Shallots (see page 121), to serve			

1 Put the steaks in a single layer in a shallow glass dish. Mix together the ale or stout, sugar, Worcestershire sauce and oil in a jug and pour over the steaks. Turn to coat, then cover and leave to marinate in the fridge for at least 2 hours, or overnight.

2 Remove the steaks from the dish, reserving the marinade. Crush the peppercorns in a pestle and mortar, sprinkle evenly over the steaks and press down well.

3 Barbecue the steaks for 4–5 minutes on each side, depending how well you like them cooked, drizzling with the marinade. Serve with Fire-roasted Shallots.

Preparation time: 10 minutes + 2 hours marinating
Cooking time: 10 minutes

Thai-spiced Steak

Serves 4

	METRIC	IMPERIAL	AMERICAN
Thin sirloin steaks, about 100 g/4 oz each	8	8	8
Roasted peanuts, finely chopped	50 g	2 oz	½ cup
Spring onions (scallions), finely sliced	6	6	6
Piece of fresh root ginger, peeled and grated	5 cm	2 in	2 in
Red chilli, seeded and chopped	1	1	1
Sesame oil	30 ml	2 tbsp	2 tbsp
Dark brown sugar	30 ml	2 tbsp	2 tbsp
Ground cumin	5 ml	1 tsp	1 tsp
Sherry vinegar	15 ml	1 tbsp	1 tbsp
Rice wine or dry sherry	150 ml	¼ pint	⅔ cup
Chopped fresh coriander (cilantro)	45 ml	3 tbsp	3 tbsp
Chicken stock	120 ml	4 fl oz	½ cup
Juice of 1 lime			
Creamy Coconut Rice (see page 120), to serve			

1 Put the steaks in a shallow glass dish. Mix together the peanuts, spring onions, ginger, chilli, oil, sugar, cumin, vinegar and 30 ml/2 tbsp of the wine or sherry. Spread over both sides of the steaks, cover and marinate in the fridge for at least 4 hours, or overnight.

2 Remove the steaks and put the marinade in a small pan with the remaining wine or sherry, stock and lime juice. Bring to the boil and simmer for about 6 minutes, until reduced to a thick sauce.

3 Barbecue the beef for about 4 minutes on each side, depending on how you like your meat. Serve the beef with a little of the sauce spooned over and the rest served separately. Accompany with Creamy Coconut Rice.

 Preparation time: 20 minutes + 4 hours marinating
Cooking time: 14 minutes

Boozy Barbecue Steaks

Kangaroo meat, renowned for its gamey flavour, is enjoyed in South Australia and the Northern Territories. Rump steaks make a delicious alternative in this simple recipe if your butcher is out of kangaroo.

Serves 4

	METRIC	IMPERIAL	AMERICAN
Kangaroo or rump steaks, 2.5 cm/1 in thick	4	4	4
Brandy	90 ml	6 tbsp	6 tbsp
Dark Muscovado sugar	15 ml	1 tbsp	1 tbsp
Dark soy sauce	30 ml	2 tbsp	2 tbsp
Tomato purée (paste)	5 ml	1 tsp	1 tsp
Freshly ground black pepper			
Fire-baked Jackets (see page 114) and a mixed salad, to serve			

1   Make a few small cuts along the fatty edge of the steaks to prevent them curling up during cooking, then place in a shallow dish.

2   Mix together the brandy, sugar, soy sauce, tomato purée and pepper in a small bowl, stirring to dissolve the sugar. Pour over the steaks, turning them to coat completely. Cover and marinate in the fridge for at least 2 hours or overnight.

3   Barbecue the steaks over hot coals for 3 minutes on each side. Move them to a slightly cooler part of the barbecue and cook for a further 3–6 minutes on each side, depending how well you like your meat cooked, basting occasionally with the marinade.

4   Serve the steaks on warmed plates with Fire-baked Jackets and a mixed salad.

 Preparation time: 10 minutes + 2 hours marinating
Cooking time: 15 minutes

Chargrilled Kangaroo

Since kangaroo steaks are less readily available in the UK, you may like to try this with beef.

Serves 4

	METRIC	IMPERIAL	AMERICAN
Kangaroo steaks, about 175 g/6 oz each	4	4	4
Salt and freshly ground black pepper			
Dry red wine	120 ml	4 fl oz	½ cup
Sunflower oil	30 ml	2 tbsp	2 tbsp
Small onion, chopped	1	1	1
Juniper berries, crushed	2.5 ml	½ tsp	½ tsp
Sprigs of fresh thyme	2	2	2
Pesto Baby Potatoes (see page 119), to serve			

1   Lightly season the steaks with salt and ground black pepper and place in a shallow dish.

2   Whisk together the red wine, oil, chopped onion and crushed juniper berries in a jug. Strip the leaves from the sprigs of thyme, add and stir well.

3   Pour the mixture over the steaks. Cover and marinate in the fridge for at least 4 hours or overnight, turning a couple of times.

4   Barbecue the steaks for about 8 minutes on each side, depending on how well done you like your meat, basting frequently.

5   Move the steaks to the coolest part of the barbecue to allow the meat to rest for 5 minutes. Serve hot with Pesto Baby Potatoes.

 Preparation time: 10 minutes + 4 hours marinating
Cooking time: 16 minutes

Greek Beef with Tzatziki

Serves 4

	METRIC	IMPERIAL	AMERICAN
Sirloin or rump steaks, 2.5 cm/1 in thick	4	4	4
Olive oil	75 ml	5 tbsp	5 tbsp
Lemon juice	45 ml	3 tbsp	3 tbsp
Chopped fresh oregano	30 ml	2 tbsp	2 tbsp
Cucumber	1	1	1
Salt	2.5 ml	½ tsp	½ tsp
Greek-style plain yoghurt	300 ml	½ pint	1¼ cups
Garlic clove, crushed	1	1	1
Chopped fresh mint	30 ml	2 tbsp	2 tbsp
Freshly ground black pepper			
Chargrilled Aubergines (see page 113) and Hot Bread with Herb Butter (see page 134), to serve			

1 Place the steaks in a shallow dish. Mix together 60 ml/ 4 tbsp of the olive oil, the lemon juice and oregano and pour over the steaks. Leave to marinate for at least 2 hours.

2 For the Tzatziki, halve, seed and finely dice the cucumber and put in a sieve (strainer). Sprinkle with the salt and leave over a bowl to drain for 20 minutes. Pat dry on kitchen paper (paper towels) and tip into a bowl.

3 Add the yoghurt to the cucumber with the remaining olive oil, the garlic, mint and pepper. Mix together, then cover and chill in the fridge until ready to serve.

4 Remove the steaks from the marinade and barbecue for 5–8 minutes on each side until cooked to your liking. Season with salt and pepper.

5 Serve the steaks with the Tzatziki, Chargrilled Aubergines and Hot Bread with Herb Butter.

Preparation time: 15 minutes + 2 hours marinating
Cooking time: 15 minutes

Steak and Onion Baguettes

Serves 4

	METRIC	IMPERIAL	AMERICAN
Fillet steaks, 175 g/6 oz each	4	4	4
Sunflower oil	45 ml	3 tbsp	3 tbsp
Red wine vinegar	5 ml	1 tsp	1 tsp
Large onion, sliced	1	1	1
Caster (superfine) sugar	5 ml	1 tsp	1 tsp
Butter, softened	40 g	1½ oz	3 tbsp
Wholegrain mustard	10 ml	2 tsp	2 tsp
Chopped fresh parsley	30 ml	2 tbsp	2 tbsp
Salt and freshly ground black pepper			
Mini baguettes	4	4	4
Little Gem lettuce leaves, to serve			

1 Put the steaks in a shallow dish. Mix together 30 ml/2 tbsp of the oil with the vinegar and brush over both sides of the steaks. Leave to marinate for at least 15 minutes.

2 Meanwhile, heat the remaining oil in a frying pan (skillet) and gently cook the onion for 5 minutes. Sprinkle over the sugar and cook for a further 5 minutes or until the onion is very soft and golden brown.

3 Beat the softened butter together with the wholegrain mustard, chopped parsley and a little salt and pepper.

4 Cook the steaks on the barbecue for 8–12 minutes, until cooked to your liking, turning once. Remove and cut into thin strips.

5 Cut open the baguettes and line each with a few lettuce leaves. Fill with hot onions and steak, then dot with the mustard and parsley butter. Serve straight away as the butter begins to melt.

Preparation time: 15 minutes + 15 minutes marinating
Cooking time: 12 minutes

Hot and Spicy Mixed Satay

Serves 4–6

	METRIC	IMPERIAL	AMERICAN
Rump steak	350 g	12 oz	12 oz
Chicken breasts, skinned and boned	2	2	2
Raw prawns (shrimp)	12	12	12
Garlic cloves, crushed	2	2	2
Dark brown sugar	30 ml	2 tbsp	2 tbsp
Ground coriander (cilantro)	10 ml	2 tsp	2 tsp
Ground cumin	10 ml	2 tsp	2 tsp
Ground turmeric	2.5 ml	½ tsp	½ tsp
Lemon juice	30 ml	2 tbsp	2 tbsp
Can of coconut milk	400 ml	14 fl oz	1 large
Salt and freshly ground black pepper			
Roasted unsalted peanuts	100 g	4 oz	1 cup
Thai red or green curry paste	30 ml	2 tbsp	2 tbsp
Lemon or lime wedges, to garnish			

1 Cut the steak into long strips about 2.5 cm/1 in wide. Put the chicken breasts between two sheets of oiled clingfilm (plastic wrap). Gently bash with a meat mallet or rolling pin until 1 cm/½ in thick. Cut into strips the same size as the steak.

2 Peel and devein the prawns, leaving the tails attached. Put the meat and prawns in a shallow glass dish.

3 Mix 1 garlic clove, 15 ml/1 tbsp of the sugar, the coriander, cumin, turmeric, 15 ml/1 tbsp of the lemon juice, 45 ml/ 3 tbsp of the coconut milk, and the salt and pepper together to make a paste.

4 Spread the spice paste over the meat and prawns. Cover and leave to marinate for at least 1 hour.

5 For the peanut sauce, put the peanuts in a food processor with the curry paste, the second clove of garlic, the remaining sugar and lemon juice and half the coconut milk. Blend until fairly smooth.

6 Add the rest of the coconut milk and blend again until well mixed. Transfer to a small pan and simmer very gently for 10 minutes, stirring occasionally. Leave to cool, then spoon into a serving bowl.

7 Thread all the pieces of meat and the prawns on to soaked wooden skewers. Barbecue the prawns for about 4 minutes, the steak for 5 minutes and the chicken for 7 minutes, until cooked, turning once.

8 Garnish with lemon or lime wedges and serve with the peanut sauce.

 Preparation time: 25 minutes + 1 hour marinating
Cooking time: 7 minutes

Marinated Fillet Steaks with Black Olive Butter

Topping barbecued steak with a slice or two of flavoured butter is a wonderful way of jazzing it up. It's also great for chops, jacket potatoes and vegetables.

Serves 4

	METRIC	IMPERIAL	AMERICAN
Fillet steaks, about 200 g/7 oz each	4	4	4
Red wine	150 ml	¼ pint	⅔ cup
Unsalted butter, softened	100 g	4 oz	½ cup
Stoned (pitted) black olives, finely chopped	25 g	1 oz	2 tbsp
Freshly ground black pepper			
Olive oil	30 ml	2 tbsp	2 tbsp

1 Place the steaks in a shallow dish, pour over the wine and leave to marinate for 1 hour at room temperature, turning occasionally.

2 Blend together the butter, olives and black pepper. Shape into a roll and wrap in clingfilm (plastic wrap). Chill until firm.

3 Remove the steaks from the wine and pat dry on kitchen paper (paper towels). Lightly brush both sides with olive oil.

4 Barbecue for about 8 minutes, turning once, until cooked to your liking. Slice the butter and serve each steak with a couple of slices on top.

 Preparation time: 20 minutes + 1 hour marinating
Cooking time: 8 minutes

Try these flavoured butter combinations for a change. Blend with 100 g/4 oz/½ cup unsalted butter, then shape into a roll and wrap in clingfilm (plastic wrap). Chill before slicing.

Hot Green Peppercorn: 30 ml/2 tbsp drained green peppercorns in brine and a dash of Tabasco sauce.

Thyme and Mustard: 15 ml/1 tbsp chopped fresh thyme leaves, 15 ml/1 tbsp Dijon mustard, salt and freshly ground black pepper.

Sun-dried Tomato and Basil: 1 finely chopped garlic clove, 8 sun-dried tomatoes in oil, finely chopped, 45 ml/3 tbsp chopped fresh basil leaves, salt and freshly ground black pepper.

Coriander and Chilli: 1 red chilli, seeded and finely chopped, 30 ml/2 tbsp chopped fresh coriander (cilantro), salt and freshly ground black pepper.

Steak Ribbon Skewers

Serves 4

	METRIC	IMPERIAL	AMERICAN
Rump steak	350 g	12 oz	12 oz
Paprika	15 ml	1 tbsp	1 tbsp
A pinch of cayenne			
Ground cumin	5 ml	1 tsp	1 tsp
Dried thyme	2.5 ml	½ tsp	½ tsp
Salt and freshly ground black pepper			
Olive oil	30 ml	2 tbsp	2 tbsp
Small button mushrooms	175 g	6 oz	6 oz
Red (bell) pepper	1	1	1
Hot Bread with Herb Butter (see page 134), to serve			

1 Trim any fat off the steak, then gently bash with a meat mallet or rolling pin to flatten slightly.

2 Mix together the seasonings and 15 ml/1 tbsp of the olive oil. Spread over both sides of the steak, then cut into long 2.5 cm/1 in wide strips.

3 Trim off the mushroom stalks. Halve, core and seed the red pepper and cut into bite-sized chunks.

4 Thread the meat like a concertina on to metal skewers, alternating with the mushrooms and pepper. Lightly brush the vegetables with the remaining oil.

5 Barbecue for 5–6 minutes, turning several times during cooking. Serve with Hot Bread with Herb Butter.

 Preparation time: 15 minutes
Cooking time: 6 minutes

LAMB

With such vast open grazing lands, it's hardly surprising that lamb and beef are the most popular meats in Australia. While barbecue recipes for beef are based around just a few suitable cuts, lamb is a far more versatile meat. In this section, you'll find recipes for a range of cuts, including minced (ground) lamb, fillet, cutlets, leg and shoulder.

Lamb is at its best when still slightly pink in the centre, so when cooking steaks and chops, make sure they're medium-sized and of even thickness. If they are too thin, the meat may be dry; too thick, and the inside will remain very rare when the outside is browned.

Butterflied Leg of Lamb

*Ask your butcher to prepare the lamb for you by 'butterflying',
i.e. boning and opening it out flat, so that it cooks evenly on
the barbecue.*

Serves 4–6

	METRIC	IMPERIAL	AMERICAN
Leg of lamb, butterflied	1.75 kg	4 lb	4 lb
Chopped fresh parsley	30 ml	2 tbsp	2 tbsp
Chopped fresh rosemary	15 ml	1 tbsp	1 tbsp
Dried mixed herbs	10 ml	2 tsp	2 tsp
Garlic cloves, crushed	2	2	2
Olive oil	60 ml	4 tbsp	4 tbsp
Red wine vinegar	30 ml	2 tbsp	2 tbsp
Salt and freshly ground black pepper			
Fresh Mint and Apple Relish (see page 139), to serve			

1 Lay the meat skin-side down and make small shallow cuts
all over the surface.

2 Mix together the fresh and dried herbs, garlic, olive oil,
vinegar, salt and pepper to make a paste. Spread over both
sides of the lamb. Cover and marinate in the fridge for at
least 3 hours or overnight.

3 Use four long skewers to hold the meat flat in the butterfly
position while cooking. Barbecue skin-side down for about
20 minutes until well browned and crisp, then turn and
cook for a further 12–15 minutes.

4 Allow the meat to rest for 10 minutes before carving into
slices. Serve with Fresh Apple and Mint Relish.

 Preparation time: 15 minutes + 3 hours marinating
Cooking time: 35 minutes

Rosemary Lamb Skewers

Serves 4

	METRIC	IMPERIAL	AMERICAN
Lamb fillet	350 g	12 oz	12 oz
Sweet sherry	60 ml	4 tbsp	4 tbsp
Clear honey	30 ml	2 tbsp	2 tbsp
Lemon juice	15 ml	1 tbsp	1 tbsp
Sunflower oil	15 ml	1 tbsp	1 tbsp
Salt and freshly ground black pepper			
Sprigs of fresh rosemary	4	4	4
Lambs' liver, thickly sliced	175 g	6 oz	6 oz
Lambs' kidneys	4	4	4
Rashers (slices) of streaky bacon, rinded	8	8	8
Barbecued Mixed Vegetables (see page 117), to serve			

1   Trim the fat from the lamb fillet and cut into 2.5 cm/1 in cubes. Mix the sherry, honey, lemon juice, oil, salt and pepper. Add the lamb and marinate for at least 1 hour.

2   Meanwhile, strip the leaves from the rosemary and reserve. Soak the stems in cold water.

3   Cut the lambs' liver into 2.5 cm/1 in cubes. Add to the lamb fillet and leave to marinate for a further 30 minutes.

4   Halve and skin the kidneys, then snip out the central cores with scissors. Wrap a rasher of bacon around each one.

5   Remove the meat and liver from the marinade and thread on to the rosemary stems, alternating with the bacon-wrapped kidneys.

6   Sprinkle the rosemary leaves over the hot coals to make rosemary-scented smoke. Barbecue the lamb skewers for about 15 minutes, turning and basting several times. Serve with Barbecued Mixed Vegetables.

 Preparation time: 20 minutes + 1½ hours marinating
Cooking time: 15 minutes

Sweet and Spicy Lamb Ribs

Serves 4

	METRIC	IMPERIAL	AMERICAN
Breast of lamb	700 g	1½ lb	1½ lb
Garlic clove, crushed	1	1	1
Tomato ketchup (catsup)	30 ml	2 tbsp	2 tbsp
Maple syrup or clear honey	30 ml	2 tbsp	2 tbsp
Dark soy sauce	30 ml	2 tbsp	2 tbsp
Sherry vinegar	30 ml	2 tbsp	2 tbsp
Worcestershire sauce	15 ml	1 tbsp	1 tbsp
Dijon mustard	10 ml	2 tsp	2 tsp
Chilli powder	2.5 ml	½ tsp	½ tsp
Ground ginger	2.5 ml	½ tsp	½ tsp
Salt and freshly ground black pepper			

1 Using a sharp knife, cut the lamb into individual ribs and put into a large shallow bowl.

2 Mix together the remaining ingredients and spoon over the meat. Turn the ribs to coat evenly. Cover and marinate in the fridge for at least 2 hours, or overnight.

3 Barbecue the ribs for about 15 minutes, turning and basting frequently with the reserved marinade until well browned and cooked through.

 Preparation time: 10 minutes + 2 hours marinating
Cooking time: 15 minutes

Minted Lamb Burgers

These moist burgers, served in pitta breads with Feta cheese, have a distinctly Greek flavour.

Serves 4

	METRIC	IMPERIAL	AMERICAN
Lean minced (ground) lamb	450 g	1 lb	1 lb
Small onion, very finely chopped	1	1	1
Chopped fresh mint	30 ml	2 tbsp	2 tbsp
Pine nuts	50 g	2 oz	½ cup
Salt and freshly ground black pepper			
Pitta or flatbreads	4	4	4
Feta cheese, crumbled	50 g	2 oz	¼ cup
Salad leaves, to serve			

1 Put the minced lamb, onion, mint and pine nuts in a bowl and mix together, seasoning well with salt and pepper.

2 Divide the mixture into four and shape into oval burgers. Chill in the fridge for at least 30 minutes or until required.

3 Barbecue for about 6 minutes on each side until browned and the juices run clear when pierced with a sharp knife or skewer.

4 Warm the pitta or flatbreads on the barbecue for about 1 minute. Split open the bread and fill with a few salad leaves, the burgers and a little crumbled cheese.

 Preparation time: 15 minutes + 30 minutes chilling
Cooking time: 12 minutes

Chilli Lamb Cutlets with Mango Relish

Serves 4

	METRIC	IMPERIAL	AMERICAN
Lamb cutlets	8	8	8
Chilli sauce	10 ml	2 tsp	2 tsp
Sunflower oil	15 ml	1 tbsp	1 tbsp
Ripe mango	1	1	1
Cider vinegar	30 ml	2 tbsp	2 tbsp
Light brown sugar	45 ml	3 tbsp	3 tbsp
Grated fresh root ginger	15 g	½ oz	1 tbsp
Salt and freshly ground black pepper			

1   Place the lamb cutlets in a shallow dish. Mix together the chilli sauce and oil and lightly brush over both sides. Cover and keep in the fridge until ready to cook.

2   To make the relish, halve, peel and dice the mango, cutting the flesh away from the stone (pit).

3   Put the cider vinegar, sugar and ginger into a pan and heat gently until the sugar dissolves. Add the mango and cook for about 3 minutes, until soft. Season with a little salt and pepper.

4   Barbecue the lamb for 5–6 minutes on each side, depending on thickness, until cooked to your liking. Serve with warm Mango Relish.

Preparation time: 15 minutes
Cooking time: 15 minutes

Lamb and Caramelised Kumquat Kebabs

Serves 4

	METRIC	IMPERIAL	AMERICAN
Small orange	1	1	1
Lean lamb	450 g	1 lb	1 lb
Cooked long-grain rice	100 g	4 oz	1 cup
Chopped fresh mint	30 ml	2 tbsp	2 tbsp
Salt and freshly ground black pepper			
Kumquats	12	12	12
Clear honey	15 ml	1 tbsp	1 tbsp
Unsalted butter, melted	15 g	½ oz	1 tbsp
Sprigs of fresh mint, to garnish			

1 Pare a thin strip of rind from the orange and roughly chop. Cube the lamb and put in a food processor with the orange rind and rice. Process until fairly smooth. Add the chopped mint, salt and pepper and process for a few more seconds.

2 Divide the mixture into 16 and mould in oval shapes on to four lightly oiled metal skewers, alternating with the kumquats, so that there are four lamb balls and three kumquats on each. Place in a shallow dish.

3 Squeeze the juice from the orange and mix with the honey and butter. Place the kebabs in a shallow dish and drizzle over the orange glaze.

4 Barbecue the kebabs for 10–12 minutes, turning frequently and brushing with the orange glaze, until the lamb is well browned and cooked and the kumquats lightly caramelised. Serve garnished with sprigs of fresh mint.

 Preparation time: 15 minutes
Cooking time: 10 minutes

Souvlakia

The yoghurt in these Greek kebabs makes the lamb meltingly tender and succulent.

Serves 4

	METRIC	IMPERIAL	AMERICAN
Shoulder or leg of lamb	900 g	2 lb	2 lb
Small lemons	2	2	2
Greek-style plain yoghurt	150 ml	1/4 pint	2/3 cup
Olive oil	30 ml	2 tbsp	2 tbsp
Chopped fresh oregano	30 ml	2 tbsp	2 tbsp
Garlic clove, crushed	1	1	1
Freshly grated nutmeg	1.5 ml	1/4 tsp	1/4 tsp
Salt and freshly ground black pepper			
Red onions	2	2	2
Sprigs of fresh oregano, to garnish			
Roasted Peppers with Feta Cheese (see page 118), to serve			

1 Trim the lamb of any excess fat and cut into 2.5 cm/1 in chunks. Put into a bowl.

2 Finely grate the rind and squeeze the juice from one of the lemons. Reserve 15 ml/1 tbsp of the juice.

3 Mix the rind and remaining juice with the yoghurt, 15 ml/1 tbsp of the oil, the oregano, garlic, nutmeg, salt and pepper. Pour over the lamb, turning to coat well. Cover and marinate in the fridge for at least 2 hours, or overnight.

4 Peel the onions, then cut each into eight wedges, keeping the root end intact. Cut the whole lemon into eight wedges. Mix the reserved oil and lemon juice together and brush over the onion and lemon wedges.

5 Thread the lamb cubes, onion and lemon wedges on to four metal skewers and barbecue for 10–12 minutes, turning occasionally and brushing the lamb with the yoghurt marinade, until the lamb and onions are cooked.

6 Place the kebabs on warmed plates and garnish with sprigs of oregano. Serve with Roasted Peppers with Feta Cheese.

 Preparation time: 15 minutes + 2 hours marinating
Cooking time: 10 minutes

Crispy Coated Chops

Serves 4

	METRIC	IMPERIAL	AMERICAN
Lamb chops, about 175 g/6 oz each	4	4	4
Fresh white breadcrumbs	50 g	2 oz	1 cup
Medium oatmeal	45 ml	3 tbsp	3 tbsp
Salt and freshly ground black pepper			
Egg, beaten	1	1	1
Sprigs of flat leaf parsley, to garnish			
Chilli-glazed Corn Cobs (see page 115), to serve			

1 Trim any excess fat from the lamb chops. Mix the breadcrumbs, oatmeal, salt and pepper together.

2 Brush the chops with beaten egg, then dip into the breadcrumb mixture to coat. Chill in the fridge for 30 minutes.

3 Barbecue for about 6 minutes on each side, depending on thickness, until done to your liking. Garnish with flatleaf parsley and serve with Chilli-glazed Corn Cobs.

 Preparation time: 15 minutes + 30 minutes chilling
Cooking time: 12 minutes

Liver and Onion Kebabs with Balsamic Glaze

Serves 4

	METRIC	IMPERIAL	AMERICAN
Baby button onions	12	12	12
Thickly sliced lambs' liver	450 g	1 lb	1 lb
Rashers (slices) of thin-cut streaky bacon, rinded	6	6	6
Butter	25 g	1 oz	2 tbsp
Balsamic vinegar	30 ml	2 tbsp	2 tbsp
Salt and freshly ground black pepper			
Chopped fresh parsley	30 ml	2 tbsp	2 tbsp

1 Put the baby onions in a small pan. Pour over enough boiling water to cover and simmer for 4 minutes. Drain and rinse under cold running water, then peel off the skins.

2 Cut the liver into 2.5 cm/1 in cubes. Cut the bacon rashers in half, then roll up. Thread on to four metal skewers, alternating with the onions.

3 Melt the butter over a low heat and stir in the balsamic vinegar and a little salt and pepper. Brush all over the kebabs.

4 Barbecue the kebabs for about 8 minutes, turning occasionally and brushing with the glaze, until lightly browned and cooked through. Sprinkle with chopped parsley before serving.

Preparation time: 15 minutes
Cooking time: 12 minutes

Barbecued Rack of Lamb with Orange and Thyme

Serves 4–6

	METRIC	IMPERIAL	AMERICAN
Racks of lamb, each with 6–7 cutlets	2	2	2
Salt and freshly ground black pepper			
Olive oil	45 ml	3 tbsp	3 tbsp
Chopped fresh thyme	30 ml	2 tbsp	2 tbsp
Finely grated rind and juice of 1 orange			
Pesto Baby Potatoes (see page 119), to serve			

1 Trim the lamb racks of excess fat, but keep a thin covering so that the meat stays moist during cooking. Sprinkle all over with salt and pepper.

2 Whisk together the olive oil, chopped thyme, orange rind and juice and pour over the lamb, turning to coat. Cover and marinate in the fridge for at least 2 hours, or overnight.

3 Barbecue for about 15 minutes, turning several times during cooking and basting with the marinade, until the outside is well browned and the inside still slightly pink.

4 Cover and leave to rest for 10 minutes. Carve into cutlets and serve with Pesto Baby Potatoes.

 Preparation time: 10 minutes + 2 hours marinating
Cooking time: 15 minutes

Herby Lamb Pockets with Mustard Butter

Serves 4

	METRIC	IMPERIAL	AMERICAN
Lamb loin chops	8	8	8
Unsalted butter	15 g	½ oz	1 tbsp
Shallots, finely chopped	2	2	2
Celery stick, finely chopped	1	1	1
Button mushrooms, chopped	50 g	2 oz	2 oz
Chopped fresh mint	15 ml	1 tbsp	1 tbsp
Fresh white breadcrumbs	25 g	1 oz	½ cup
Grated nutmeg	1.5 ml	¼ tsp	¼ tsp
Salt and freshly ground black pepper			
Butter, softened	50 g	2 oz	¼ cup
Dijon mustard	15 ml	1 tbsp	1 tbsp
Lemon juice	10 ml	2 tsp	2 tsp
Crunchy Red Coleslaw (see page 129), to serve			

1   Cut pockets in the chops by slicing horizontally into the meat until you reach the bone.

2   Melt the butter in a saucepan and gently cook the shallots and celery for 5 minutes. Add the mushrooms and cook for a further 3 minutes, until soft. Leave to cool.

3   Stir the mint, breadcrumbs, nutmeg, salt and pepper into the vegetables. Spoon the stuffing into the lamb pockets.

4   Beat the butter, mustard and lemon juice and season with salt and pepper. Thinly spread half over the chops.

5   Barbecue the chops for about 6 minutes on each side, until browned on the outside and just cooked through. Top with the remaining butter and serve with Crunchy Red Coleslaw.

Preparation time: 15 minutes
Cooking time: 12 minutes

Lamb Steaks with Pomegranates

Serves 4

	METRIC	IMPERIAL	AMERICAN
Lamb leg steaks	4	4	4
Pomegranates	2	2	2
Freshly ground pink peppercorns			
Onion, thinly sliced	1	1	1
New Potato Salad (see page 122), to serve			

1 Place the lamb in a single layer in a shallow dish. Cut the pomegranates in half. Pick out the seeds from one of the halves and keep for garnishing. Squeeze the juice from the other three using a lemon squeezer and pour over the lamb.

2 Grind a little pink pepper over the steaks, then tuck the onion slices under. Cover and marinate in the fridge for at least 2 hours, or overnight.

3 Remove the lamb from the marinade and barbecue for 6–8 minutes each side, depending on thickness, until cooked to your liking, brushing with the pomegranate marinade frequently.

4 Sprinkle the lamb steaks with the reserved pomegranate seeds and serve with New Potato Salad.

Preparation time: 15 minutes + 2 hours marinating
Cooking time: 15 minutes

Peppered Lamb Cutlets with Citrus Glaze

Use lemon or lime marmalade instead of orange, if you prefer.

Serves 4

	METRIC	IMPERIAL	AMERICAN
Lamb cutlets	8	8	8
Black or tropical peppercorns	15 ml	1 tbsp	1 tbsp
Fine-cut orange marmalade	45 ml	3 tbsp	3 tbsp
Lemon juice	15 ml	1 tbsp	1 tbsp
Sunflower oil	10 ml	2 tsp	2 tsp
Salt	1.5 ml	¼ tsp	¼ tsp
Barbecued Mixed Vegetables (see page 117), to serve			

1 Trim any excess fat from the cutlets. Crush the peppercorns with a pestle and mortar, or the end of a rolling pin.

2 Put the marmalade, lemon juice and oil in a small pan and heat gently until melted. Brush all over both sides of the cutlets, then sprinkle over the peppercorns and a little salt and press down firmly.

3 Barbecue the cutlets for 5–7 minutes on each side, depending on thickness, until cooked to your liking. Serve with Barbecued Mixed Vegetables.

Preparation time: 10 minutes
Cooking time: 15 minutes

Lamb Steaks with Mint Pesto

Serves 4

	METRIC	IMPERIAL	AMERICAN
Lamb leg steaks	4	4	4
Salt and freshly ground black pepper			
Olive oil	150 ml	¼ pint	⅔ cup
Balsamic vinegar	15 ml	1 tbsp	1 tbsp
Pine nuts	50 g	2 oz	½ cup
Fresh mint leaves	25 g	1 oz	½ cup
Freshly grated Parmesan cheese	50 g	2 oz	½ cup
Sprigs of fresh mint, to garnish			
Fruity Rice Salad (see page 126), to serve			

1   Lightly season the lamb steaks with salt and pepper and place in a shallow non-metallic dish. Mix together 30 ml/ 2 tbsp of the oil and the balsamic vinegar and brush over both sides of the steaks.

2   For the pesto, put the pine nuts in a food processor with the mint and about 60 ml/4 tbsp of the oil. Process until finely chopped.

3   Tip into a bowl or jug and stir in the remaining olive oil and grated Parmesan cheese.

4   Barbecue the lamb for 7–8 minutes on each side, depending on thickness, until cooked to your liking. Drizzle the pesto over the steaks and garnish with fresh mint. Serve with Fruity Rice Salad.

Preparation time: 10 minutes
Cooking time: 15 minutes

PORK

No barbecue would be complete without sizzling sausages, often referred to by Australians as 'snags' or 'snaggers'. You'll also find recipes here for a whole range of tender pork cuts such as fillet, loin, chops, bacon and gammon.

Pork must be thoroughly cooked so that the juices run clear when pierced through the thickest part of the meat. Test only when you think it is done, as repeatedly piercing the meat will dry it out. To guide you, press the meat with the back of a fork. If it is soft, with plenty of give, it is still rare. When well done, the meat will feel firm.

Position the meat at a suitable distance from the heat so that it can cook through to the centre as the outside browns. If it's too hot, the outside may char before the middle is cooked. The rack should be placed about 10 cm/4 in away from the coals. If necessary, reduce the temperature by raising the rack or spreading out the coals.

Glazed Gammon with Spiced Pineapple and Apple Rings

Serves 4

	METRIC	IMPERIAL	AMERICAN
Gammon steaks, about 175 g/6 oz each	4	4	4
Clear honey	15 ml	1 tbsp	1 tbsp
Sunflower oil	10 ml	2 tsp	2 tsp
Wholegrain mustard	15 ml	1 tbsp	1 tbsp
Apple juice	30 ml	2 tbsp	2 tbsp
Eating (dessert) apples	2	2	2
Can of pineapple rings, drained	200 g	7 oz	1 small
Unsalted butter, melted	25 g	1 oz	2 tbsp
Demerara sugar	30 ml	2 tbsp	2 tbsp
Ground cinnamon	1.5 ml	¼ tsp	¼ tsp
Ground ginger	1.5 ml	¼ tsp	¼ tsp
Ground allspice	1.5 ml	¼ tsp	¼ tsp

1 Make small cuts in the fat around the gammon steaks with a pair of scissors or a sharp knife to stop them curling up during cooking.

2 Mix together the honey, oil, mustard and apple juice. Brush the mixture over both sides of the gammon steaks.

3 Core the apples and cut into thick slices. Pat the apple and pineapple slices dry on kitchen paper (paper towels), then brush with butter. Mix together the sugar and spices and dip in the fruit to coat.

4 Barbecue the gammon for about 4 minutes on each side, basting occasionally with any remaining honey mixture.

5 Cook the fruit rings beside the gammon for about 2 minutes on each side. Top the gammon with the barbecued fruit and serve hot.

 Preparation time: 15 minutes
Cooking time: 12 minutes

Pork and Peanut Satay Sticks

Serves 4

	METRIC	IMPERIAL	AMERICAN
Pork fillet	450 g	1 lb	1 lb
Sunflower oil	15 ml	1 tbsp	1 tbsp
Small onion, finely chopped	1	1	1
Garlic clove, crushed	1	1	1
Red chilli, seeded and finely chopped	1	1	1
Light brown sugar	10 ml	2 tsp	2 tsp
Dark soy sauce	30 ml	2 tbsp	2 tbsp
Lime juice	30 ml	2 tbsp	2 tbsp
Water	60 ml	4 tbsp	4 tbsp
Smooth peanut butter	75 ml	5 tbsp	5 tbsp
Chopped fresh coriander (cilantro)	30 ml	2 tbsp	2 tbsp
A sprig of fresh coriander and lime wedges, to garnish			
Creamy Coconut Rice (see page 120), to serve			

1 Trim any fat from the meat. Slice into thin strips, then thread concertina-style on to soaked wooden skewers. Put in a shallow dish.

2 Heat the oil in a small pan and cook the onion over a low heat for 10 minutes, or until soft. Add the garlic and chilli and cook for a further minute, stirring all the time.

3 Add the sugar, soy sauce, lime juice and water to the pan. Simmer gently for a few seconds, then remove from the heat. Stir in the peanut butter and chopped coriander.

4 Brush one-third of the peanut sauce over the pork. Barbecue for about 10 minutes, or until lightly browned and cooked through.

5 Spoon the remaining peanut sauce into a serving bowl and
garnish with a sprig of coriander. Serve the pork skewers
with the peanut dip and lime wedges to squeeze over.
Accompany with Creamy Coconut Rice.

 Preparation time: 20 minutes
Cooking time: 10 minutes

Chilli Pork and Cheese Burgers

Serves 4

	METRIC	IMPERIAL	AMERICAN
Minced (ground) pork	*700 g*	*1½ lb*	*1½ lb*
Garlic clove, crushed	*1*	*1*	*1*
Sweet chilli sauce	*30 ml*	*2 tbsp*	*2 tbsp*
Chopped fresh coriander (cilantro)	*30 ml*	*2 tbsp*	*2 tbsp*
Salt and freshly ground black pepper			
Mozzarella cheese	*50 g*	*2 oz*	*2 oz*
Burger buns	*4*	*4*	*4*

1 Put the minced pork, garlic, chilli sauce, coriander, salt and
pepper in a bowl and mix together thoroughly.

2 Divide the mixture into four equal portions. Cut the cheese
into four pieces and mould each portion of meat around a
piece of cheese, then flatten slightly into a burger. Chill for
1 hour if time allows.

3 Barbecue the burgers for about 15 minutes, turning once,
until cooked through. Serve straight away in toasted burger
buns.

 Preparation time: 15 minutes + 1 hour chilling
Cooking time: 15 minutes

Sweet and Spicy Ham and Pineapple Kebabs

Use a 350 g/12 oz/large can of pineapple cubes instead of the fresh pineapple, if preferred.

Serves 4

	METRIC	IMPERIAL	AMERICAN
Medium sherry	100 ml	3½ fl oz	scant ½ cup
Piece of fresh root ginger, peeled and grated	2.5 cm	1 in	1 in
Garlic cloves, crushed	2	2	2
Cardamom pods, crushed	4	4	4
Star anise, lightly crushed	1	1	1
Clear honey	30 ml	2 tbsp	2 tbsp
Black peppercorns	4	4	4
Thick ham steak	450 g	1 lb	1 lb
Small pineapple	1	1	1

1 Put the sherry, ginger, garlic, cardamoms, star anise, honey and black pepper into a pan. Gently warm over a low heat for a minute, but do not boil. Remove from the heat, cover and leave to infuse for 20 minutes.

2 Meanwhile, cut the ham steak into 2.5 cm/1 in cubes and place in a bowl. Strain over the sherry mixture, turning the ham to coat. Cover and leave to marinate in the fridge for at least 1 hour, or overnight.

3 Lay the pineapple on its side. Slice off the top and bottom ends, then cut off the coarse skin and 'woody' eyes. Cut the pineapple into 2.5 cm/ 1 in thick slices. Remove the centre core of each slice with an apple corer, then cut the pineapple rings into chunks.

4 Remove the ham from the marinade and thread on to metal skewers, alternating with the pineapple chunks.

5 Barbecue the kebabs for about 8 minutes, turning and basting frequently with the marinade. Serve straight away.

 Preparation time: 20 minutes + 1 hour marinating
Cooking time: 8 minutes

Oaty Bacon Burgers with Tangy Tomato Baste

Serves 4

	METRIC	IMPERIAL	AMERICAN
Collar bacon, trimmed and cubed	350 g	12 oz	12 oz
Dried mixed herbs	2.5 ml	½ tsp	½ tsp
Freshly ground black pepper			
Jumbo or porridge oats	50 g	2 oz	½ cup
Egg, beaten	1	1	1
Tomato ketchup (catsup)	45 ml	3 tbsp	3 tbsp
Olive oil	5 ml	1 tsp	1 tsp
Worcestershire sauce	5 ml	1 tsp	1 tsp
Made English mustard	2.5 ml	½ tsp	½ tsp

1 Put the bacon, herbs and black pepper in a food processor and process the mixture until coarsely chopped.

2 Transfer the mixture to a bowl. Add the oats and egg and mix together. Divide into four equal pieces and shape each into a burger. Chill for 1 hour if time allows.

3 Mix together the tomato ketchup, oil, Worcestershire sauce and mustard. Brush over the burgers and barbecue for about 5 minutes on each side, or until cooked through.

 Preparation time: 15 minutes + 1 hour chilling
Cooking time: 10 minutes

Devilled Bacon, Kidney and Mushroom Brochettes

Hot spicy sauces, known as 'devils', were popular in Britain in the 18th and 19th centuries and were taken to Australia by British settlers.

Serves 4

	METRIC	IMPERIAL	AMERICAN
Butter	25 g	1 oz	2 tbsp
Small onion, finely chopped	1	1	1
Can of chopped tomatoes	200 g	7 oz	1 small
White wine vinegar	15 ml	1 tbsp	1 tbsp
Made English mustard	2.5 ml	½ tsp	½ tsp
Light brown sugar	10 ml	2 tsp	2 tsp
Salt and freshly ground black pepper			
Rashers (slices) of smoked streaky bacon, rinded	8	8	8
Lambs' kidneys	4	4	4
Baby button mushrooms	16	16	16
Orange juice	60 ml	4 tbsp	4 tbsp
Chilli-glazed Corn Cobs (see page 115), to serve			

1 Melt the butter in a small pan and gently fry (sauté) the onion for 5 minutes until soft. Add the tomatoes, vinegar, mustard, sugar, salt and pepper. Simmer for 5 minutes until fairly thick. Leave to cool.

2 Cut each bacon rasher in half and roll tightly. Cut the kidneys in half, cut out the white core and discard. Cut each kidney half into two. Trim the mushrooms.

3 Push a bacon roll, a kidney, then a mushroom on to a skewer. Repeat the sequence, then repeat to make another seven skewers. Brush all over with about half of the devilled sauce.

4 Barbecue for about 7 minutes, turning occasionally. Stir
the orange juice into the remaining sauce and simmer for
3 minutes. Serve two brochettes per person with the sauce
and Chilli-glazed Corn Cobs.

Preparation time: 15 minutes
Cooking time: 10 minutes

Red-cooked Pork

Serves 4

	METRIC	IMPERIAL	AMERICAN
Boned leg or shoulder of pork	750 g	1¾ lb	1¾ lb
Piece of fresh root ginger, peeled and grated	2.5 cm	1 in	1 in
Garlic clove, crushed	1	1	1
Sesame oil	10 ml	2 tsp	2 tsp
Dark soy sauce	60 ml	4 tbsp	4 tbsp
Dark brown sugar	15 ml	1 tbsp	1 tbsp
Dry sherry	60 ml	4 tbsp	4 tbsp
Hoisin sauce	30 ml	2 tbsp	2 tbsp
Ground star anise	1.5 ml	¼ tsp	¼ tsp
Marinated Cucumber (see page 140), to serve			

1 Trim the pork of any fat, then cut into 2.5 cm/1 in cubes.
Mix together the ginger, garlic, sesame oil, soy sauce, sugar,
sherry, hoisin sauce and star anise in a bowl.

2 Add the pork to the marinade and stir to coat thoroughly.
Cover and marinate in the fridge for at least 4 hours.

3 Thread the pork on to four metal skewers. Barbecue for
about 15 minutes, turning and brushing with any
remaining marinade until browned and cooked through.
Serve with Marinated Cucumber.

Preparation time: 10 minutes + 4 hours marinating
Cooking time: 15 minutes

Prune and Bacon Snags

Here, sausages, or 'snags', are split and filled with prunes, then wrapped with bacon to hold them together while cooking.

Serves 4

	METRIC	IMPERIAL	AMERICAN
Thick pork sausages	450 g	1 lb	1 lb
Stoned (pitted) prunes, halved	100 g	4 oz	²/₃ cup
Rashers (slices) of streaky bacon	4	4	4
Tomato purée (paste)	10 ml	2 tsp	2 tsp
Malt vinegar	15 ml	1 tbsp	1 tbsp
Dark brown sugar	15 ml	1 tbsp	1 tbsp
English mustard powder	5 ml	1 tsp	1 tsp
Vegetable stock	120 ml	4 fl oz	¹/₂ cup
Salt and freshly ground black pepper			
Fire-baked Jackets (see page 114), to serve			

1   Prick the sausages with a fine skewer. Place in a saucepan and pour over enough cold water to cover. Bring to the boil, reduce the heat and simmer for 5 minutes. Drain and leave to cool.

2   When cold, split the sausages in half, taking care not to cut all the way through. Fill each with two or three prune halves.

3   Cut the rind off the bacon, then place on a board and gently stretch each rasher with the back of a knife. Cut each rasher in half and wrap around the sausages. Secure with a wooden cocktail stick (toothpick).

4   Meanwhile, put all remaining ingredients in a small pan and bring to the boil. Turn down the heat and simmer for 3 minutes, stirring all the time. Brush the sausages with the sauce.

5 Barbecue for about 7 minutes, turning several times and brushing generously with the sauce during cooking. Remove the cocktail sticks and serve with Fire-baked Jackets.

 Preparation time: 15 minutes
Cooking time: 7 minutes

Apricot-glazed Pork Chops

Serves 4

	METRIC	IMPERIAL	AMERICAN
Pork chops or loin steaks, 2.5 cm/1 in thick	4	4	4
Apricot preserve	45 ml	3 tbsp	3 tbsp
Maple syrup or clear honey	30 ml	2 tbsp	2 tbsp
Dark brown sugar	15 ml	1 tbsp	1 tbsp
Cider vinegar	30 ml	2 tbsp	2 tbsp
Wholegrain mustard	10 ml	2 tsp	2 tsp
Coriander (cilantro) seeds, crushed	10 ml	2 tsp	2 tsp
Salt and freshly ground black pepper			

1 Trim the pork chops of any excess fat and place in a shallow non-metallic dish.

2 Put the apricot preserve, maple syrup or honey, sugar, vinegar, mustard, coriander seeds, salt and pepper in a saucepan. Heat gently to melt, then simmer for 2 minutes. Leave to cool.

3 Brush over both sides of the pork chops. Barbecue for 12–15 minutes on each side until cooked through and lightly browned.

 Preparation time: 10 minutes
Cooking time: 30 minutes

Fiery Spare Ribs

Serves 4–6

	METRIC	IMPERIAL	AMERICAN
Short Chinese pork spare ribs	1.5 kg	3 lb	3 lb
Garlic clove, crushed	1	1	1
Chilli powder	5 ml	1 tsp	1 tsp
Piece of fresh root ginger, peeled and grated	2.5 cm	1 in	1 in
Tomato purée (paste)	30 ml	2 tbsp	2 tbsp
White wine vinegar	30 ml	2 tbsp	2 tbsp
Dark brown sugar	30 ml	2 tbsp	2 tbsp
Hoisin sauce	15 ml	1 tbsp	1 tbsp
Dark soy sauce	30 ml	2 tbsp	2 tbsp
French mustard	15 ml	1 tbsp	1 tbsp
Salt and freshly ground pepper			

1   Trim any fat from the ribs and put them in a large saucepan. Cover with water, bring to the boil, reduce the heat and simmer gently for 45 minutes. Drain and transfer to a large shallow dish or roasting tin (pan).

2   Mix together all the remaining ingredients in a jug and pour over the ribs, turning them to coat in the sauce. Leave to marinate for 30 minutes.

3   Barbecue the ribs for about 25 minutes, turning and basting with the marinade several times during cooking, until the pork is tender and a rich brown colour.

Preparation time: 50 minutes + 30 minutes marinating
Cooking time: 25 minutes

Smoked Pork and Gingered Fruit Skewers

Serves 4

	METRIC	IMPERIAL	AMERICAN
Smoked pork loin	700 g	1½ lb	1½ lb
Can of pineapple pieces in natural juice	200 g	7 oz	1 small
Preserved ginger, finely chopped	15 ml	1 tbsp	1 tbsp
Syrup from preserved ginger	30 ml	2 tbsp	2 tbsp
Cider vinegar	15 ml	1 tbsp	1 tbsp
Light brown sugar	15 ml	1 tbsp	1 tbsp
Freshly ground black pepper			
Ripe nectarines	2	2	2

1   Cut the pork into 2.5 cm/1 in chunks and put in a shallow dish. Drain the pineapple, pouring the juice into a small pan. Add the ginger, ginger syrup, vinegar and sugar. Simmer for 5 minutes or until reduced by half. Leave to cool.

2   Season the pork with a little pepper. Pour over the syrup and turn to coat well. Cover and leave to marinate for 1 hour.

3   Meanwhile, halve and stone (pit) the nectarines, then cut into chunks. Add to the marinade with the pineapple pieces and stir to coat.

4   Thread the pork and fruit pieces alternately on to soaked wooden skewers. Barbecue for about 7 minutes, turning once or twice during cooking and brushing with the marinade.

 Preparation time: 15 minutes + 1 hour marinating
Cooking time: 7 minutes

Pork Fillets with Peach Stuffing

If the peaches are difficult to peel, put them in a bowl of boiling water for 1 minute, then cool under cold water.

Serves 4

	METRIC	IMPERIAL	AMERICAN
Butter	25 g	1 oz	2 tbsp
Shallot, finely chopped	1	1	1
Small celery stick, finely chopped	1	1	1
Small peaches, peeled and chopped	2	2	2
Chopped fresh parsley	30 ml	2 tbsp	2 tbsp
Fresh white breadcrumbs	40 g	1½ oz	¾ cup
Freshly grated nutmeg	1.5 ml	¼ tsp	¼ tsp
Salt and freshly ground black pepper			
Pork fillets, about 225 g/8 oz each	2	2	2
Slices of prosciutto or Parma ham	6	6	6
Olive oil	15 ml	1 tbsp	1 tbsp
Pesto Baby Potatoes (see page 119), to serve			

1 To make the stuffing, melt the butter in a saucepan and gently fry (sauté) the chopped shallot and celery for 5 minutes until soft. Leave to cool.

2 Add the chopped peaches to the shallot mixture with the parsley, breadcrumbs and nutmeg. Season and mix well.

3 Make a cut along the length of each pork fillet, slicing halfway through. Open out and cover with oiled clingfilm (plastic wrap). Gently beat out with a rolling pin until about 5 mm/¼ in thick.

4 Spoon the filling down the centre of each pork fillet, then fold over the sides to enclose. Wrap three overlapping slices of prosciutto around each roll. Secure with soaked wooden cocktail sticks (toothpicks.).

5 Brush all over with oil and barbecue for about 25 minutes, turning occasionally, until the juices run clear when the meat is pierced with a fine skewer and the outside is crisp and brown.

6 Leave to rest at the side of the barbecue for 5 minutes. Remove the cocktail sticks and slice. Serve with Pesto Baby Potatoes.

Preparation time: 20 minutes
Cooking time: 30 minutes

POULTRY

Chicken is probably the most versatile of barbecue
foods. Flavourings can range from the simplest
drumsticks, briefly marinated, to the hot and spicy
Thai-inspired dishes favoured in Australian cuisine.
You'll also find recipes in this chapter for turkey and
duck. Baste turkey frequently as it tends to dry out
quickly. Duck is a fattier meat, so needs little attention
during cooking.
Always make sure that poultry is thoroughly cooked.
Avoid pricking the meat often during cooking as
precious juices will escape. Test the thickest part of the
meat when you think it's done; the juices should run
clear when pierced. Take care, though, not to overcook
poultry, or it will become dry and tasteless. Remove
from the heat as soon as it is ready.

Seared Chicken with a Spiced Yoghurt Crust

Yoghurt makes a great marinade as it tenderises meat and forms a crust on the outside which helps keep in the juices.

Serves 4

	METRIC	IMPERIAL	AMERICAN
Chicken breasts, skinned and boned	4	4	4
Coriander (cilantro) seeds	10 ml	2 tsp	2 tsp
Mild curry paste	10 ml	2 tsp	2 tsp
Garlic clove, crushed	1	1	1
Thick plain yoghurt	300 ml	½ pint	1¼ cups
Salt and freshly ground black pepper			
Mango and Guava Relish (see page 139), to serve			

1 Prick the chicken breasts all over with a fork or fine skewer, then place in a shallow non-metallic dish.

2 Crush the coriander seeds in a mortar with a pestle. Mix with the curry paste, garlic and yoghurt, seasoning with salt and pepper.

3 Pour the yoghurt marinade over the chicken, and turn to coat thoroughly. Cover and leave to marinate in the fridge for at least 1 hour or overnight.

4 Remove the chicken from the marinade and barbecue for about 8 minutes on each side until cooked through. Serve with Mango and Guava Relish.

 Preparation time: 10 minutes + 1 hour marinating
Cooking time: 16 minutes

Chicken Thighs with Lemon Grass and Ginger Dipping Sauce

This delicious chicken dish comes from Vietnam, where lemon grass is a commonly used ingredient. If you have difficulty finding it, the finely grated rind of a lemon can be substituted.

Serves 4

	METRIC	IMPERIAL	AMERICAN
Garlic cloves, finely chopped	3	3	3
Shallot, peeled and chopped	1	1	1
Lemon grass stalks, bruised and finely chopped	2	2	2
Caster (superfine) sugar	45 ml	3 tbsp	3 tbsp
Nam pla (fish sauce)	60 ml	4 tbsp	4 tbsp
Sesame or sunflower oil	15 ml	1 tbsp	1 tbsp
A little water			
Small chicken thighs, skinned and boned	8	8	8
Salt and freshly ground black pepper			
Piece of fresh root ginger, peeled and grated	2.5 cm	1 in	1 in
Red chilli, seeded and finely chopped	1	1	1
Juice of 1 lime			
Rice or sherry vinegar	30 ml	2 tbsp	2 tbsp
Sesame Noodle Salad (see page 124), to serve			

1 Put two of the garlic cloves, the chopped shallot, lemon grass and 15 ml/1 tbsp of the sugar in a mortar and crush to a paste with a pestle. Mix in 15 ml/1 tbsp of the nam pla, the oil and 15 ml/1 tbsp water.

2 Put the chicken thighs in a single layer in a shallow non-metallic dish. Season with a little salt and pepper, then spread with the paste. Cover and leave to marinate in the fridge for 1 hour, or overnight if preferred.

3 For the Ginger Dipping Sauce, crush the remaining garlic and sugar, the ginger and chilli in a mortar with a pestle. Mix in the rest of the nam pla, lime juice and vinegar. Transfer to a small bowl.

4 Barbecue the chicken thighs for about 8 minutes on each side, or until lightly browned and cooked through. Serve with the Ginger Dipping Sauce and Sesame Noodle Salad.

 Preparation time: 20 minutes + 1 hour marinating
Cooking time: 16 minutes

Quick Chicken Pesto

When preparation time is at a premium, these tasty drumsticks are the perfect answer; and they taste wonderful, so don't be surprised if guests ask you for the recipe!

 Serves 4

	METRIC	IMPERIAL	AMERICAN
Chicken drumsticks	8	8	8
Red or green pesto sauce	60 ml	4 tbsp	4 tbsp

1 Make three or four shallow slashes in the skin of each drumstick and place in a single layer in a shallow dish.

2 Spoon over the pesto sauce, turning the chicken to coat well. If time allows, cover and leave to marinate in the fridge for at least 15 minutes.

3 Barbecue the chicken for about 20 minutes, turning several times, until well browned and cooked through.

 Preparation time: 5 minutes + 15 minutes marinating
Cooking time: 20 minutes

Barbecued Chicken with Caramelised Lemons

Serves 4

	METRIC	IMPERIAL	AMERICAN
Whole chicken	1.6 kg	3½ lb	3½ lb
Medium onion, peeled	1	1	1
Unsalted butter, softened	50 g	2 oz	¼ cup
Lemons, thickly sliced	2	2	2
Juice of 1 lemon			
Salt and freshly ground black pepper			
Bay leaves	2	2	2
Sunflower oil	30 ml	2 tbsp	2 tbsp
Barbecued Mixed Vegetables (see page 117), to serve			

1   Put the chicken on a lightly greased roasting rack or in a disposable baking dish. Push the onion inside the chicken.

2   Melt half the butter in a frying pan (skillet) and cook the lemon slices until softened and slightly caramelised. Mix the remaining butter with 15 ml/1 tbsp of the lemon juice and the salt and pepper.

3   Carefully loosen the skin around the chicken breast and push the lemon slices, bay leaves and flavoured butter under. Tie the chicken legs together with string.

4   Mix together the oil and the remaining lemon juice and brush all over the chicken. Cook in a covered barbecue, following the manufacturer's instructions, for about 1½ hours or until well browned and cooked through.

5   Allow the chicken to rest for 10 minutes, before cutting into quarters and serving. Serve with Barbecued Mixed Vegetables.

 Preparation time: 20 minutes
Cooking time: 1½ hours

Chicken and Melted Cheese Parcels

Serves 4

	METRIC	IMPERIAL	AMERICAN
Large boneless chicken thighs	4	4	4
Butter, softened	25 g	1 oz	2 tbsp
Fresh thyme leaves	15 ml	1 tbsp	1 tbsp
Salt and freshly ground black pepper			
Mozzarella cheese	150 g	5 oz	5 oz
Olive oil	15 ml	1 tbsp	1 tbsp
Pasta and Tamarillo Salad (see page 125), to serve			

1   Put the chicken thighs on a board, skin-side down. Mix together the butter, thyme, salt and pepper and thinly spread a little over the chicken. Cut the cheese into four equal pieces and place one in the middle of each thigh.

2   Roll up tightly and secure each with two or three soaked wooden cocktail sticks (toothpicks). Chill in the fridge for at least 30 minutes, or overnight if preferred.

3   Brush the outside of the thighs with olive oil, then barbecue skin-side down for about 12 minutes, until the skin is crisp and brown. Turn and cook for a further 8 minutes or until cooked through.

4   Remove the cocktail sticks and serve the chicken with Pasta and Tamarillo Salad.

 Preparation time: 15 minutes + 30 minutes chilling
Cooking time: 20 minutes

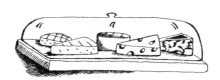

Turkey Steaks with Apricot Glaze

Serves 4

	METRIC	IMPERIAL	AMERICAN
Turkey breast steaks	4	4	4
Salt and freshly ground black pepper			
Apricot jam (conserve)	100 g	4 oz	⅓ cup
Lemon juice	15 ml	1 tbsp	1 tbsp
Red or white white wine	30 ml	2 tbsp	2 tbsp
Ground ginger	1.5 ml	¼ tsp	¼ tsp
New Potato Salad (see page 122), to serve			

1   Lightly season both sides of the turkey breast steaks with salt and pepper and put in a shallow glass dish.

2   Put the apricot jam and lemon juice in a small pan and gently heat until the jam melts. Remove from the heat and sieve (strain) into a small bowl. Stir in the wine and ground ginger. Leave to cool.

3   Pour the Apricot Glaze over the turkey steaks, turning them to coat completely. Cover and leave to marinate in the fridge for 1 hour.

4   Remove the turkey from the marinade and barbecue for about 5 minutes on each side, basting frequently with the reserved marinade during cooking. Serve with New Potato Salad.

 Preparation time: 10 minutes + 1 hour marinating
Cooking time: 10 minutes

Turkey and Spicy Snag Kebabs

Makes 8

	METRIC	IMPERIAL	AMERICAN
Turkey breast fillet	450 g	1 lb	1 lb
Chorizo sausage	225 g	8 oz	8 oz
Olive oil	45 ml	3 tbsp	3 tbsp
Red wine vinegar	15 ml	1 tbsp	1 tbsp
Garlic clove, crushed	1	1	1
Red chilli, seeded and finely chopped	1	1	1
Freshly ground black pepper			
Red or yellow (bell) pepper	1	1	1
Bay leaves, cut in half	8	8	8

1 Cut the turkey breast into 2.5 cm/1 in cubes and the chorizo sausage into 2.5 cm/1 in lengths.

2 Mix together the oil, wine vinegar, garlic, chilli and black pepper in a bowl. Add the turkey and sausage pieces and turn to coat with the marinade. Cover and chill for at least 1 hour.

3 Halve and seed the pepper, then cut into 2.5 cm/1 in chunks. Thread the turkey and sausage pieces on to metal skewers, alternating with the pepper and bay leaves.

4 Barbecue the kebabs for about 12 minutes, or until the turkey is cooked through and browned, turning and basting frequently with the marinade.

 Preparation time: 15 minutes + 1 hour marinating
Cooking time: 12 minutes

Crispy Spiced Quail

Serves 4

	METRIC	IMPERIAL	AMERICAN
Oven-ready quail	4	4	4
Salt			
Green ginger wine	100 ml	3½ fl oz	scant ½ cup
Garlic cloves, crushed	2	2	2
Lemon juice	15 ml	1 tbsp	1 tbsp
Sesame oil	15 ml	1 tbsp	1 tbsp
Szechwan peppercorns, crushed	15 ml	1 tbsp	1 tbsp
Star anise, crushed	2	2	2
Dried red chilli, seeded and crushed	1	1	1
Sesame Noodle Salad (see page 124), to serve			

1 Using poultry shears or sharp scissors, cut down both sides of each quail's backbone and remove. Snip the wishbone in half. Open out on a board and press down hard on the breastbone with the heel of your hand to flatten. Cut away the rib cage and discard. Season with salt, rubbing well into the skin.

2 Mix together the ginger wine, garlic, lemon juice, sesame oil, crushed peppercorns, star anise and chilli. Place the quail in a shallow dish and pour over the marinade, turning to coat. Cover and marinate in the fridge for at least 2 hours, or overnight.

3 Remove the quail from the marinade and barbecue for about 25 minutes, turning several times and basting with the marinade during cooking. Serve with Sesame Noodle Salad.

Preparation time: 25 minutes + 2 hours marinating
Cooking time: 25 minutes

Chinese Crispy Duck with Plum Compôte

Serves 4

	METRIC	IMPERIAL	AMERICAN
Duck legs	4	4	4
Dark soy sauce	30 ml	2 tbsp	2 tbsp
Dark brown sugar	50 g	2 oz	¼ cup
Salt	1.5 ml	¼ tsp	¼ tsp
Plums, stoned (pitted) and chopped	450 g	1 lb	1 lb
Unsalted butter	15 g	½ oz	1 tbsp
Star anise	1	1	1
Piece of fresh root ginger, peeled and grated	2.5 cm	1 in	1 in
Finely grated rind and juice of 1 orange			
Shredded spring onions (scallions), to garnish			
Marinated Cucumber (see page 140), to serve			

1 Prick the skin of the duck legs all over. Place in a large bowl and cover with boiling water. Leave for 1 minute, then drain and pat dry on kitchen paper (paper towels).

2 Mix together the soy sauce, 30 ml/2 tbsp of the sugar and the salt. Rub over the skins of the duck. Leave to marinate for 30 minutes, or overnight if preferred.

3 Put the plums in a saucepan with the butter, star anise, ginger, orange rind and juice and the remaining sugar. Bring to the boil, then turn down the heat and gently simmer for 20 minutes, until soft. Remove the star anise and spoon the compôte into a serving bowl.

4 Barbecue the duck legs for 15–20 minutes on each side until cooked through, well browned and very crisp. Garnish with shredded spring onions and serve with the Plum Compôte and Marinated Cucumber.

 Preparation time: 20 minutes + 30 minutes marinating
Cooking time: 40 minutes

Chicken and Smoky Bacon Burgers

Serves 4

	METRIC	IMPERIAL	AMERICAN
Minced (ground) chicken	350 g	12 oz	12 oz
Rashers (slices) of smoked streaky bacon, rinded and finely chopped	4	4	4
Small red onion, finely chopped	1	1	1
Fresh white breadcrumbs	50 g	2 oz	1 cup
Dried tarragon	5 ml	1 tsp	1 tsp
Egg, beaten	1	1	1
Dijon mustard	15 ml	1 tbsp	1 tbsp
Salt and freshly ground black pepper			
Sunflower oil	15 ml	1 tbsp	1 tbsp
Burger buns	4	4	4
Shredded lettuce, sliced tomatoes and mayonnaise, to serve			

1 Put the chicken in a large bowl with the bacon, onion, breadcrumbs, tarragon, egg, mustard, salt and pepper. Mix together thoroughly.

2 Divide the mixture into four equal portions, then shape into burgers. Chill in the fridge for 20 minutes.

3 Lightly brush the burgers with oil and barbecue for about 7 minutes on each side, depending on thickness, or until cooked through.

4 Briefly toast the buns on the barbecue, place a burger in each and serve with shredded lettuce, sliced tomatoes and mayonnaise.

 Preparation time: 10 minutes + 20 minutes chilling
Cooking time: 14 minutes

Sticky Chicken Drumsticks with Garlic Dip

Serves 4

	METRIC	IMPERIAL	AMERICAN
Chicken drumsticks	8	8	8
Piece of fresh root ginger, peeled and grated	2.5 cm	1 in	1 in
Dark soy sauce	45 ml	3 tbsp	3 tbsp
Thick honey	45 ml	3 tbsp	3 tbsp
Sweet chilli sauce	15 ml	1 tbsp	1 tbsp
Juice of 1 lemon			
Mayonnaise	120 ml	4 fl oz	½ cup
Greek-style plain yoghurt	120 ml	4 fl oz	½ cup
Garlic cloves, crushed	2	2	2
Salt and freshly ground black pepper			

1 Make two or three shallow slashes through the skin of each drumstick with a sharp kife. Put in a shallow dish, large enough to hold them in a single layer.

2 Mix together the ginger, soy sauce, honey, chilli sauce and two-thirds of the lemon juice. Pour over the chicken and turn to coat thoroughly. Cover and leave to marinate in the fridge for at least 2 hours, or overnight.

3 Meanwhile, make the Garlic Dip. Mix together the mayonnaise, yoghurt, garlic and the remaining lemon juice. Season well with salt and pepper. Transfer to a small serving bowl, cover and chill until needed.

4 Barbecue the drumsticks for about 20–25 minutes, turning frequently and basting with marinade, until browned all over and cooked through. Serve with the Garlic Dip.

 Preparation time: 15 minutes + 2 hours marinating
Cooking time: 25 minutes

Sizzling Chicken Skewers with Grilled Bananas

Cooking chicken on lemon grass stalks gives it a wonderful aromatic flavour.

Serves 4

	METRIC	IMPERIAL	AMERICAN
Chicken breasts	350 g	12 oz	12 oz
Lemon grass stalks, about 15 cm/6 in long	4	4	4
Finely grated rind and juice of 1 lime			
Peanut (groundnut) or sunflower oil	30 ml	2 tbsp	2 tbsp
Red chilli, seeded and finely chopped	1	1	1
Garlic clove, crushed	1	1	1
Chopped fresh coriander (cilantro)	45 ml	3 tbsp	3 tbsp
Muscovado sugar	15 ml	1 tbsp	1 tbsp
Medium bananas, unpeeled	4	4	4
Coconut cream	90 ml	6 tbsp	6 tbsp
Sprigs of fresh coriander, to garnish			

1   Cut the chicken breasts into strips. Trim the lemon grass stalks to equal lengths, then finely chop the trimmings and mix with the lime juice and rind, peanut or sunflower oil, chilli, garlic, chopped coriander and sugar.

2   Thread the chicken on to the lemon grass stalks and place in a shallow dish. Pour over the marinade, turning to coat thoroughly. Cover and leave to marinate in the fridge for at least 1 hour.

3   Cut the unpeeled bananas in half lengthwise. Brush the coconut cream over the cut side of each banana.

4   Barbecue the chicken skewers for about 10 minutes, or until the chicken is cooked through, turning frequently and basting.

5 Meanwhile, barbecue the bananas, cut side down, for about 4 minutes until well browned, then turn and cook for 3 minutes until soft.

6 Garnish with sprigs of fresh coriander and serve with the bananas, drizzled with any remaining coconut cream.

 Preparation time: 20 minutes + 1 hour marinating
Cooking time: 10 minutes

Chilli Coconut Chicken

This quick and simple coconut milk marinade tenderises and flavours the chicken and keeps it moist and succulent.

Serves 6

	METRIC	IMPERIAL	AMERICAN
Skinless chicken breasts	6	6	6
Salt and freshly ground black pepper			
Red chilli, seeded and finely chopped	1	1	1
Spring onions (scallions), finely sliced	6	6	6
Can of coconut milk	400 ml	14 fl oz	1 large
Green Papaya and Carrot Salad (see page 123), to serve			

1 Make three or four shallow slashes in each chicken breast, lightly season with salt and pepper and place in a single layer in a non-metallic dish.

2 Mix together the red chilli, spring onions and coconut milk and pour over the chicken, turning to coat well. Cover and marinate in the fridge for 1 hour.

3 Remove the chicken from the marinade and barbecue for about 8 minutes on each side, turning several times and basting with the marinade, until cooked through. Serve with Green Papaya and Carrot Salad.

 Preparation time: 10 minutes + 1 hour marinating
Cooking time: 16 minutes

Chargrilled Chicken with Creamy Cheese

Serves 4

	METRIC	IMPERIAL	AMERICAN
Boneless chicken breasts	4	4	4
Full-fat cream cheese	100 g	4 oz	½ cup
Garlic clove, crushed	1	1	1
Chopped fresh parsley	15 ml	1 tbsp	1 tbsp
Salt and freshly ground black pepper			
Rashers (slices) of streaky bacon, rinded	8	8	8
Olive oil	45 ml	3 tbsp	3 tbsp
White wine vinegar	10 ml	2 tsp	2 tsp
Dijon mustard	5 ml	1 tsp	1 tsp
Pesto Baby Potatoes (see page 119), to serve			

1 Using a sharp knife, cut a large pocket in each chicken breast. Mix together the cream cheese, garlic, parsley, salt and pepper. Divide equally between the chicken pockets.

2 Stretch the bacon, using the back of a knife. Wrap two rashers around each stuffed chicken breast and secure with a soaked wooden cocktail stick (toothpick).

3 Mix together the oil, vinegar and mustard and brush all over the bacon-wrapped chicken.

4 Barbecue for about 10 minutes on each side until the chicken is cooked through and the bacon is crisp. Remove the cocktail sticks and serve with Pesto Baby Potatoes.

Preparation time: 15 minutes
Cooking time: 20 minutes

Spatchcocked Chicken with Lemon and Mustard Butter

Serves 4

	METRIC	IMPERIAL	AMERICAN
Poussins, about 700 g/1½ lb each	2	2	2
Butter, softened	50 g	2 oz	¼ cup
Wholegrain mustard	30 ml	2 tbsp	2 tbsp
Finely grated rind and juice of 1 lemon			
Clear honey	15 ml	1 tbsp	1 tbsp
Salt and freshly ground black pepper			
Thin lemon slices, to garnish			
Fruity Rice Salad (see page 126), to serve			

1   Spatchcock the poussins: using poultry shears or a sharp heavy knife, cut down one side of the backbone. Cut down the other side of the backbone and remove.

2   Snip the wishbone in half. Place the bird on a board, skin-side up, and press down hard on the breastbone with the heel of your hand to break and flatten it.

3   Mix the butter, mustard, lemon rind, honey, salt and pepper together. Gently ease up the skin of the breast and legs of the poussin and push in the flavoured butter.

4   Thread two metal or soaked wooden skewers crosswise through each bird to hold it flat. Sprinkle with lemon juice.

5   Barbecue the poussins for about 25 minutes, turning once, until browned and the juices from the thigh run clear when pierced with a skewer.

6   Add the lemon slices to the barbecue for the last 5 minutes to brown slightly. Remove the skewers from the poussins and split each one in half along the breastbone. Garnish with lemon slices and serve with Fruity Rice Salad.

 Preparation time: 25 minutes
Cooking time: 25 minutes

Spinach and Almond-stuffed Chicken Legs

Serves 4

	METRIC	IMPERIAL	AMERICAN
Chicken legs	4	4	4
Baby spinach leaves, washed	50 g	2 oz	2 oz
Egg yolk	1	1	1
Greek-style plain yoghurt	45 ml	3 tbsp	3 tbsp
Ground almonds	25 g	1 oz	¼ cup
Unblanched almonds, chopped and toasted	25 g	1 oz	¼ cup
Grated nutmeg	1.5 ml	¼ tsp	¼ tsp
Salt and freshly ground black pepper			
Sunflower oil	30 ml	2 tbsp	2 tbsp

1   Find the end of the thigh bone of each of the chicken legs and, using a sharp knife, scrape away the meat until the whole bone is exposed. Cut through the joint to remove the bone.

2   Put the spinach in a saucepan and gently cook for about 2 minutes until wilted. Drain well and cool, then chop finely. Put in a bowl with the egg yolk, yoghurt, almonds, nutmeg, salt and pepper.

3   Mix together the stuffing until thoroughly combined, then spoon the stuffing into the thigh cavities. Fold over the skin to enclose and secure with wooden cocktail sticks (toothpicks). Brush the skins with oil and sprinkle with a little salt.

4   Barbecue for about 25 minutes, turning frequently, until the skin is crisp and browned and the chicken is cooked through.

 Preparation time: 25 minutes
Cooking time: 25 minutes

Marinated Emu with Cranberry and Wine Sauce

Use duck fillets as an alternative if your local supermarket is out of emu!

Serves 4

	METRIC	IMPERIAL	AMERICAN
Emu fillets, about 175 g/6 oz each	4	4	4
Sunflower oil	45 ml	3 tbsp	3 tbsp
Red wine	300 ml	½ pint	1¼ cups
Garlic clove, crushed	1	1	1
Dried bay leaves, crumbled	2	2	2
Salt and freshly ground black pepper			
Fresh or frozen cranberries	175 g	6 oz	6 oz
Caster (superfine) sugar	50 g	2 oz	¼ cup
Finely grated rind and juice of 1 orange			

1 Put the emu fillets in a shallow dish. Mix together the oil, 150 ml/¼ pint/⅔ cup of the wine, the garlic, bay leaves, salt and pepper and pour over the emu, turning to coat well. Cover and marinate in the fridge for at least 4 hours, or overnight.

2 Put the cranberries, sugar, orange rind and juice and the remaining wine in a saucepan and simmer, uncovered, for 20 minutes, stirring occasionally.

3 Using a slotted spoon, lift out half of the cranberries and place in a bowl. Pour the rest of the cranberries and juice into a blender and process until smooth. Return the purée and cranberries to the pan and reheat gently.

4 Remove the emu from the marinade and barbecue for about 10 minutes on each side, depending on thickness, until cooked to your liking. Serve with the Cranberry and Wine Sauce.

 Preparation time: 15 minutes + 4 hours marinating
Cooking time: 20 minutes

Spicy Turkey Meatball Sticks with Plum Tomato Salsa

Serves 4

	METRIC	IMPERIAL	AMERICAN
Minced (ground) turkey	450 g	1 lb	1 lb
Fresh white breadcrumbs	50 g	2 oz	1 cup
Egg, beaten	1	1	1
Ground cumin	5 ml	1 tsp	1 tsp
Mild chilli powder	5 ml	1 tsp	1 tsp
Ground turmeric	1.5 ml	¼ tsp	¼ tsp
Salt and freshly ground black pepper			
Plum tomatoes, peeled and chopped	6	6	6
Spring onions (scallions), finely chopped	4	4	4
Cucumber, finely chopped	¼	¼	¼
Olive oil	45 ml	3 tbsp	3 tbsp
Red wine vinegar	10 ml	2 tsp	2 tsp
Chopped fresh coriander (cilantro) or parsley	30 ml	2 tbsp	2 tbsp
Green salad, to serve			

1   Put the turkey, breadcrumbs, egg, cumin, chilli powder and turmeric in a bowl and mix together, seasoning with salt and pepper. Using wet hands, divide and shape the mixture into 20 balls. Chill in the fridge for 1 hour.

2   To make the salsa, mix the tomatoes, spring onions and cucumber together. Mix 30 ml/2 tbsp of the oil with the vinegar, chopped coriander or parsley, salt and pepper. Pour over the vegetables and mix well. Spoon into a serving bowl and chill until needed.

3   Thread the turkey balls on to four lightly oiled skewers. Lightly brush with the remaining oil.

4 Barbecue for about 10 minutes, turning carefully several
times, until browned all over and cooked through. Serve
hot with the Plum Tomato Salsa and a large green salad.

 Preparation time: 20 minutes + 1 hour chilling
Cooking time: 10 minutes

Spit-roast Duckling with Pineapple Glaze

Serves 4

	METRIC	IMPERIAL	AMERICAN
Oven-ready duckling	2 kg	4½ lb	4½ lb
Salt and freshly ground black pepper			
Pineapple juice	250 ml	8 fl oz	1 cup
Light brown sugar	45 ml	3 tbsp	3 tbsp
Light soy sauce	15 ml	1 tbsp	1 tbsp
Piece of fresh root ginger, peeled and grated	2.5 cm	1 in	1 in

1 Prick the duck all over with a sharp skewer. Season inside
and out with salt and pepper.

2 Put the pineapple juice, sugar, soy sauce and ginger in a
pan and simmer for 10 minutes, or until reduced by half.
Strain into a jug and leave to cool. Brush all over the duck.

3 When the barbecue coals are hot, move them to one side
and put a heavy-based roasting tin (pan) in the centre. Fix
the duck on to a spit or put in a roasting basket. Cover with
a foil tent or barbecue lid.

4 Barbecue over medium heat for about 2½ hours or until
the duck is cooked through. Do not open for the first
45 minutes, then baste every 15 minutes with the glaze.

 Preparation time: 15 minutes
Cooking time: 2½ hours

FISH AND SHELLFISH

Australia is famous for its rich variety and abundance of seafood. Quick to cook and needing only a short marinating time, it is ideal for impromptu barbecues. Choose firm-fleshed fish for trouble-free turning and invest in a wire basket for fragile fillets; it'll make barbecuing infinitely easier. Oily fish is particularly suitable as it doesn't dry out over direct heat; a baste or marinade is essential for white fish, or cook the fish whole as the skin keeps all the delicious juices in and protects the fish as it cooks.

Charred Tuna with Coriander and Chilli Butter

Tuna has a firm meaty texture which makes it ideal for barbecuing. It needs frequent basting during cooking to ensure it doesn't dry out. Swordfish makes a good alternative.

Serves 4

	METRIC	IMPERIAL	AMERICAN
Tuna steaks, about 150 g/5 oz each	4	4	4
Olive oil	30 ml	2 tbsp	2 tbsp
Lime or lemon juice	15 ml	1 tbsp	1 tbsp
Butter, softened	100 g	4 oz	½ cup
Chopped fresh coriander (cilantro)	15 ml	1 tbsp	1 tbsp
Green chilli, seeded and finely chopped	1	1	1
Salt and freshly ground black pepper			

1 Wash and pat the tuna steaks dry on kitchen paper (paper towels). Place in a shallow dish. Mix the oil and lime or lemon juice together and brush over both sides of the steaks. Marinade at room temperature for 20 minutes.

2 Meanwhile, mix the butter, chopped coriander and chilli together, seasoning well with salt and pepper. Shape into a roll, wrapping in clingfilm (plastic wrap) or greaseproof (waxed) paper, and chill until needed.

3 Remove the tuna from the marinade and barbecue for about 10 minutes, turning once, until cooked to your liking. Serve topped with slices of Coriander and Chilli Butter.

 Preparation time: 15 minutes + 20 minutes marinating
Cooking time: 10 minutes

Salmon Parcels with Mustard Sauce

Serves 4

	METRIC	IMPERIAL	AMERICAN
Butter, softened	50 g	2 oz	¼ cup
Finely grated rind and juice of 1 lemon			
Salt and freshly ground black pepper			
Salmon steaks, about 175 g/6 oz each	4	4	4
Dijon mustard	10 ml	2 tsp	2 tsp
Crème fraîche	150 ml	¼ pint	⅔ cup
Grilled Asparagus with Balsamic Vinegar and Herb Dressing (see page 116), to serve			

1 Mix the butter with the lemon rind and juice, salt and pepper. Cut four squares of double foil, large enough to enclose the salmon.

2 Spoon a little of the butter on to each piece of foil, top with a salmon steak, then the remaining butter. Gather the foil edges together and seal tightly.

3 For the Mustard Sauce, mix together the mustard and crème fraîche. Season with a little salt and pepper and spoon into a serving bowl.

4 Barbecue the salmon parcels for about 10 minutes, or until the fish comes away from the bone easily when tested with a fork.

5 Transfer the salmon and its buttery juices on to plates and serve with the Mustard Sauce and Grilled Asparagus with Balsamic Vinegar and Herb Dressing.

 Preparation time: 10 minutes
Cooking time: 10 minutes

Glazed Soy Salmon

The marinade of this Japanese-style dish flavours the salmon and cooks to a shiny glaze.

Serves 4

	METRIC	IMPERIAL	AMERICAN
Salmon fillets, about 175 g/6 oz each	4	4	4
Light brown sugar	15 ml	1 tbsp	1 tbsp
Light soy sauce	75 ml	5 tbsp	5 tbsp
Mirin (Japanese rice wine) or sweet sherry	75 ml	5 tbsp	5 tbsp
Piece of fresh root ginger, peeled and grated	5 cm	2 in	2 in
Garlic clove, crushed	1	1	1
Sesame Noodle Salad (see page 124), to serve			

1   Cut the salmon fillets in half lengthwise and thread a soaked wooden skewer through the length of each. Put in a single layer in a shallow dish.

2   Put the sugar, soy sauce and mirin or sherry in a small pan. Heat gently until the sugar dissolves, then simmer for about 3 minutes until reduced and syrupy. Leave to cool.

3   Put the grated ginger and crushed garlic in a mortar and pound with a pestle to a paste. Put in a fine sieve (strainer) and squeeze out as much juice as possible. Add the juice to the soy syrup.

4   Pour the syrup over the salmon, turning to coat. Cover and leave to marinate in a cool place for 30 minutes.

5   Barbecue the salmon for 5–6 minutes on each side, depending on thickness, until cooked to your liking, brushing frequently with the marinade. Serve two skewers per person with Sesame Noodle Salad.

 Preparation time: 15 minutes + 30 minutes marinating
Cooking time: 12 minutes

Seafood Platter with Saffron and Dill Mayonnaise

Serves 4

	METRIC	IMPERIAL	AMERICAN
Large mussels in shells	*450 g*	*1 lb*	*1 lb*
Small prepared fresh squid	*175 g*	*6 oz*	*6 oz*
Large raw prawns (jumbo shrimp)	*12*	*12*	*12*
Butter, melted	*25 g*	*1 oz*	*2 tbsp*
Lime juice	*15 ml*	*1 tbsp*	*1 tbsp*
Shelled scallops	*12*	*12*	*12*
Oysters, shucked	*8*	*8*	*8*
A large pinch of saffron strands			
Boiling water	*15 ml*	*1 tbsp*	*1 tbsp*
White wine vinegar	*30 ml*	*2 tbsp*	*2 tbsp*
Dijon mustard	*10 ml*	*2 tsp*	*2 tsp*
Egg yolks	*2*	*2*	*2*
Salt and freshly ground black pepper			
Light olive oil	*300 ml*	*¹/₂ pint*	*1¹/₄ cups*
Chopped fresh dill (dill weed)	*30 ml*	*2 tbsp*	*2 tbsp*
Sprigs of fresh dill and lemon wedges, to garnish			

1 Clean the mussels, discarding any that are broken or won't close when tapped. Cut the squid tubes in half and lay out flat on a board with the inside uppermost. Lightly score in a criss-cross pattern with a sharp knife. Peel and devein the prawns, leaving the tails on.

2 Mix the butter with the lime juice. Add the squid, prawns, scallops and oysters to the butter mixture and toss to coat. Thread alternately on to soaked wooden skewers.

3 For the Saffron and Dill Mayonnaise, put the saffron in a small bowl and spoon over the boiling water. Leave to infuse for 10 minutes, then strain the liquid into a food processor or blender.

4 Add the vinegar, mustard, egg yolks and seasoning and process for a few seconds. Then, with the motor still running, add the oil in a slow, steady stream to make a thick mayonnaise. Spoon into a bowl and stir in the chopped dill.

5 Barbecue the mussels over a medium heat for about 10 minutes until they open, discarding any that remain closed. After 5 minutes, add the seafood skewers. Cook for the remaining 5 minutes, turning once until just cooked through.

6 Arrange the seafood on a warmed platter and garnish with sprigs of fresh dill and lemon wedges. Serve straight away with the saffron mayonnaise.

Preparation time: 25 minutes
Cooking time: 10 minutes

Monkfish Kebabs with Coconut and Coriander

Skinned and boned salmon fillet, cod or other firm white fish can be used instead of the monkfish, if preferred.

Serves 4

	METRIC	IMPERIAL	AMERICAN
Sunflower oil	10 ml	2 tsp	2 tsp
Small onion, chopped	1	1	1
Piece of fresh root ginger, peeled and grated	2.5 cm	1 in	1 in
Canned coconut milk	150 ml	¼ pint	⅔ cup
Chopped fresh coriander (cilantro)	45 ml	3 tbsp	3 tbsp
Salt and freshly ground black pepper			
Monkfish	450 g	1 lb	1 lb
Large raw prawns (jumbo shrimp)	16	16	16

1 Heat the oil in a small pan and gently fry (sauté) the onion for 5 minutes, until soft. Add the ginger and coconut milk and simmer for about 5 minutes until thick. Leave to cool, then stir in 30 ml/2 tbsp of the chopped coriander and season with salt and pepper.

2 Meanwhile, fillet the monkfish by cutting down either side of the central bone. Cut the fish into bite-sized chunks. Peel the prawns and thread on to four metal skewers, alternating with the monkfish. Brush the coconut sauce over the kebabs, turning to coat well.

3 Barbecue for about 4 minutes on each side, according to thickness, brushing frequently with the coconut sauce, until cooked through. Serve sprinkled with the remaining chopped coriander.

Preparation time: 20 minutes
Cooking time: 8 minutes

Smoky Fish Skewers

In this recipe, breadcrumbs give the fish a crispy coating and help protect it from the heat during cooking.

Serves 4

	METRIC	IMPERIAL	AMERICAN
Smoked cod fillet	450 g	1 lb	1 lb
Garlic clove, crushed	1	1	1
Juice of ½ lemon			
Sunflower oil	30 ml	2 tbsp	2 tbsp
Chopped fresh parsley	30 ml	2 tbsp	2 tbsp
Freshly ground black pepper			
Dried breadcrumbs	60 ml	4 tbsp	4 tbsp
Rashers (slices) of smoked streaky bacon, rinded	4	4	4

1 Cut the smoked cod into large bite-sized chunks and place in a shallow dish. Mix together the garlic, lemon juice, oil, parsley and pepper, and drizzle over the fish. Coat in the breadcrumbs.

2 Gently stretch each bacon rasher with the back of a knife, cut into three pieces and roll up tightly. Thread on to four metal or soaked wooden skewers, alternating with the coated fish.

3 Barbecue for about 4 minutes on each side, depending on thickness, until the fish is cooked through and the bacon is browned and crispy.

Preparation time: 10 minutes
Cooking time: 8 minutes

Roasted Red Mullet

Serves 4

	METRIC	IMPERIAL	AMERICAN
Red mullet, cleaned and scaled	4	4	4
Fennel seeds, crushed	15 ml	1 tbsp	1 tbsp
Chopped fresh thyme	10 ml	2 tsp	2 tsp
Chopped fresh rosemary	10 ml	2 tsp	2 tsp
Garlic cloves, crushed	2	2	2
Olive oil	45 ml	3 tbsp	3 tbsp
Salt and freshly ground black pepper			
Lemon wedges and sprigs of fresh rosemary, to garnish			

1 Make two or three shallow slashes on each side of the fish with a sharp knife. Mix the fennel seeds, thyme, rosemary, garlic, 15 ml/1 tbsp of the olive oil, the salt and pepper together.

2 Divide the herb mixture between the mullet, spooning into the cavities. Leave for 30 minutes for the flavours to develop.

3 Brush the remaining olive oil over the fish and barbecue for about 12 minutes on each side, or until the skin is crisp and the fish is cooked through. Serve hot, garnished with lemon wedges and sprigs of fresh rosemary.

 Preparation time: 10 minutes + 30 minutes marinating
Cooking time: 25 minutes

Seared Barramundi with Rocket Dressing

Barramundi is a common and popular fish in Australia. If you can't find it, red mullet makes an excellent alternative. Blending olive oil with rocket gives the oil a distinctive flavour and colour.

Serves 4

	METRIC	IMPERIAL	AMERICAN
Barramundi fillets, about 100 g/4 oz each	4	4	4
Olive oil	150 ml	¼ pint	⅔ cup
Salt and freshly ground black pepper			
Rocket	40 g	1½ oz	1½ oz
Lime juice	30 ml	2 tbsp	2 tbsp

1 Brush the fish fillets on both sides with 30 ml/2 tbsp of the oil. Season with a little salt and pepper.

2 Put the rocket in a blender or food processor with the remaining oil and process until smooth. Strain through a fine sieve (strainer) into a jug, and discard the rocket purée.

3 Add the lime juice to the rocket-flavoured oil and season with salt and pepper. Whisk together with a fork.

4 Barbecue the fish skin-side down for about 6 minutes until the skin is crisp, then turn and cook for a further 3–4 minutes, or until opaque and cooked to your liking. Serve drizzled with the Rocket Dressing.

Preparation time: 10 minutes
Cooking time: 10 minutes

Abalone and Crispy Bacon Skewers

Large scallops make a good alternative to the abalone and do not need to be tenderised.

Serves 4

	METRIC	IMPERIAL	AMERICAN
Abalone, shelled	12	12	12
Olive oil	15 ml	1 tbsp	1 tbsp
White wine	60 ml	4 tbsp	4 tbsp
Wholegrain mustard	10 ml	2 tsp	2 tsp
Snipped fresh chives	30 ml	2 tbsp	2 tbsp
Salt and freshly ground black pepper			
Rashers (slices) of streaky bacon, rinded	6	6	6

1 Tenderise the abalone by beating with a wooden mallet or rolling pin. Mix together the oil, wine, mustard, chives, salt and pepper in a bowl. Add the abalone and turn to coat. Cover and marinade in a cool place for 30 minutes.

2 Remove the rind from the bacon. Stretch each rasher with the back of a knife, then cut in half. Remove the abalone from the marinade and wrap each in a piece of bacon. Thread on to a soaked wooden skewer.

3 Brush with the marinade and barbecue for about 7 minutes, turning several times until the bacon is cooked and crisp. Serve straight away.

 Preparation time: 10 minutes + 30 minutes marinating
Cooking time: 7 minutes

Swordfish Steaks with Green Olive Butter

Serves 4

	METRIC	IMPERIAL	AMERICAN
Swordfish steaks	4	4	4
Olive oil	30 ml	2 tbsp	2 tbsp
Lemon juice	15 ml	1 tbsp	1 tbsp
Unsalted butter, softened	100 g	4 oz	½ cup
Stoned (pitted) green olives, finely chopped	50 g	2 oz	⅓ cup
Chopped fresh parsley	30 ml	2 tbsp	2 tbsp
Freshly ground black pepper			
Herb-scented Ciabatta (see page 136), to serve			

1 Put the swordfish steaks in a shallow dish. Mix together the olive oil and 5 ml/1 tsp of the lemon juice and lightly brush over both sides. Leave to marinate at room temperature for 15 minutes.

2 Beat the butter, the remaining lemon juice, the olives, parsley and black pepper together. Shape into a roll and wrap in clingfilm (plastic wrap) or greaseproof (waxed) paper. Chill in the fridge until hard.

3 Barbecue the swordfish steaks for about 5 minutes on each side, until golden brown and cooked through. Top with slices of Green Olive Butter and serve with Herb-scented Ciabatta.

 Preparation time: 10 minutes + 15 minutes marinating
Cooking time: 10 minutes

Herb-cured Salmon Steaks with Caper Crème Fraîche

Serves 4

	METRIC	IMPERIAL	AMERICAN
Salmon steaks, about 175 g/6 oz each	4	4	4
Coarse sea salt	30 ml	2 tbsp	2 tbsp
Caster (superfine) sugar	15 ml	1 tbsp	1 tbsp
Chopped fresh dill (dill weed)	45 ml	3 tbsp	3 tbsp
Chopped fresh parsley	30 ml	2 tbsp	2 tbsp
Chopped fresh tarragon	30 ml	2 tbsp	2 tbsp
Carton of crème fraîche	200 ml	7 fl oz	1 small
Capers, drained	30 ml	2 tbsp	2 tbsp
Hard-boiled (hard-cooked) egg, finely chopped	1	1	1
Freshly ground black pepper			
Butter, melted	25 g	1 oz	2 tbsp

1 Put the salmon steaks in a single layer in a shallow dish. Mix together the salt, sugar, 30 ml/2 tbsp of the dill and 15 ml/1 tbsp each of parsley and tarragon. Sprinkle over both sides of the salmon, cover and leave to marinate in the fridge for at least 4 hours, or overnight.

2 Mix together the crème fraîche, capers, hard-boiled egg and the remaining dill, parsley and tarragon. Season with black pepper. Spoon into a serving dish and chill until needed.

3 Scrape the herb mixture off the salmon, then brush with melted butter. Barbecue for about 5 minutes on each side, depending on thickness, to your liking. Serve with the Caper Crème Fraîche.

 Preparation time: 10 minutes + 4 hours marinating
Cooking time: 10 minutes

Citrus Sardines in Vine Leaves

Serves 4

	METRIC	IMPERIAL	AMERICAN
Fresh sardines, cleaned	8	8	8
Lemons	2	2	2
Juice of 1 orange			
Olive oil	100 ml	3 ½ fl oz	scant ½ cup
Freshly ground black pepper			
Packet of vine leaves in brine	200 g	7 oz	7 oz
Small sprigs of fresh rosemary	8	8	8
Roasted Peppers with Feta Cheese (see page 118), to serve			

1 Using a sharp knife, remove the backbones from the sardines. Rinse in cold water and pat dry on kitchen paper (paper towels). Put in a single layer in a shallow dish.

2 Squeeze the juice from one of the lemons and mix with the orange juice, olive oil and pepper. Pour over the fish, turn to coat, cover and marinade in the fridge for at least 1 hour.

3 Halve the remaining lemon lengthwise, then thinly slice. Rinse the vine leaves well in cold water, then drain.

4 Place a sardine on top of each vine leaf. Put two halved lemon slices and a sprig of rosemary in the cavity of each fish. Wrap in the leaf, leaving the head and tail free, and secure with fine string.

5 Barbecue the sardines for about 5 minutes on each side, or until cooked through. Remove the string and serve hot with Roasted Peppers with Feta Cheese.

 Preparation time: 15 minutes + 1 hour marinating
Cooking time: 10 minutes

Thai-style Snapper

Whole red or grey mullet and tilapia are also excellent when barbecued whole in this way.

Serves 4

	METRIC	IMPERIAL	AMERICAN
Whole snapper, about 900 g/2 lb each	2	2	2
Sunflower oil	30 ml	2 tbsp	2 tbsp
Sesame oil	15 ml	1 tbsp	1 tbsp
Garlic cloves, crushed	2	2	2
Juice of 2 limes			
Chopped fresh coriander (cilantro)	30 ml	2 tbsp	2 tbsp
Piece of fresh root ginger, peeled and grated	2.5 cm	1 in	1 in
Lemon grass stalk, finely chopped	1	1	1
Green chilli, seeded and finely chopped	1	1	1
Nam pla (fish sauce)	10 ml	2 tsp	2 tsp
Caster (superfine) sugar	5 ml	1 tsp	1 tsp
Red (bell) pepper	1	1	1
Mangetout (snow peas)	200 g	7 oz	7 oz
Creamy Coconut Rice (see page 120), to serve			

1 Clean and trim the fish and make three or four shallow slashes on each side with a sharp knife. Place in a large shallow dish.

2 Mix together the oils, garlic, lime juice, coriander, ginger, lemon grass, chilli, nam pla and sugar. Reserve 45 ml/ 3 tbsp of the mixture and spoon the rest over the fish, turning to coat. Cover and marinate in a cool place for 1 hour.

3 Halve, seed and thinly slice the red pepper. Trim and cut each of the mangetout into two or three strips lengthwise. Mix with the reserved marinade sauce. Spoon the vegetables into the fish cavities.

4 Barbecue the fish, preferably in a wire basket or on a wire rack, for about 15 minutes on each side, or until cooked through. Serve with Creamy Coconut Rice.

 Preparation time: 20 minutes + 1 hour marinating
Cooking time: 30 minutes

Seared Sea Bass

Serves 4

	METRIC	IMPERIAL	AMERICAN
Sea bass fillets, about 175 g/6 oz each, unskinned	4	4	4
Salt and freshly ground black pepper			
Sunflower oil	30 ml	2 tbsp	2 tbsp
Garlic cloves, finely chopped	2	2	2
Pernod or other aniseed-flavoured alcohol	45 ml	3 tbsp	3 tbsp
Chopped fresh parsley	30 ml	2 tbsp	2 tbsp
Lemon wedges, to garnish			
Chargrilled Aubergines (see page 113), to serve			

1 Season the fish fillets on both sides with salt and pepper and put in a large shallow dish. Mix together the oil, garlic, Pernod and 15 ml/1 tbsp of the parsley. Pour over the fillets, turning to coat well. Leave to marinate for 30 minutes at room temperature.

2 Remove the fish from the marinade. Barbecue, in a wire basket if you have one, for 4–5 minutes on each side, or until just cooked through, basting with the marinade several time during cooking.

3 Place the fish fillets on warmed plates. Sprinkle with the remaining parsley and garnish with lemon wedges. Serve with Chargrilled Aubergines.

 Preparation time: 10 minutes + 30 minutes marinating
Cooking time: 10 minutes

Chunky Fish Cakes with Chilli Tomato Sauce

Serves 4

	METRIC	IMPERIAL	AMERICAN
Cod or other white fish fillet	450 g	1 lb	1 lb
Bay leaf	1	1	1
Potatoes, peeled	225 g	8 oz	8 oz
Butter	25 g	1 oz	2 tbsp
Salt and freshly ground black pepper			
Fresh coriander (cilantro)	30 ml	2 tbsp	2 tbsp
Eggs, beaten	2	2	2
Fresh white breadcrumbs	75 g	3 oz	1½ cups
Shallots, finely chopped	2	2	2
Olive oil	30 ml	2 tbsp	2 tbsp
Garlic clove, crushed	1	1	1
Red chilli, seeded and finely chopped	1	1	1
Ripe tomatoes, peeled, seeded and chopped	450 g	1 lb	1lb
Lemon juice	15 ml	1 tbsp	1 tbsp
Caster (superfine) sugar	5 ml	1 tsp	1 tsp

1 Put the fish fillets and bay leaf in a saucepan and barely cover with water. Simmer gently for about 5 minutes or until the fish is opaque. Drain the fish, remove the skin and bones, then break into large flakes.

2 Cook the potatoes in boiling salted water for about 15 minutes. Drain and mash with the butter, salt and pepper. Add the fish and coriander. Mix well, then shape into four chunky cakes.

3 Dip each fish cake into beaten egg, then into breadcrumbs, to coat. Cover and chill in the fridge for at least 1 hour.

4 Meanwhile, gently fry (sauté) the shallots in the oil for 5 minutes, until soft. Add the garlic and chilli and cook for 1 minute. Add the remaining ingredients and simmer, uncovered, for 10 minutes, stirring occasionally.

5 Barbecue the fish cakes for about 4–5 minutes on each side until browned and cooked through. Reheat the sauce and season with salt and pepper. Serve with the fish cakes.

 Preparation time: 40 minutes + 1 hour chilling
Cooking time: 10 minutes

Marinated Moreton Bay Bugs with Lemon Mayonnaise

Moreton Bay bugs and Balmain bugs are flat-headed lobsters, common in the seas surrounding Australia. Large, peeled, raw prawns (jumbo shrimp) also work well in this dish.

Serves 4

	METRIC	IMPERIAL	AMERICAN
Uncooked Moreton Bay bug tails	*8*	*8*	*8*
Olive oil	*45 ml*	*3 tbsp*	*3 tbsp*
White wine	*60 ml*	*4 tbsp*	*4 tbsp*
Shallots, finely chopped	*2*	*2*	*2*
Chopped fresh dill (dill weed)	*30 ml*	*2 tbsp*	*2 tbsp*
Salt and freshly ground black pepper			
Mayonnaise	*150 ml*	*¼ pint*	*⅔ cup*
Finely grated rind and juice of 1 small lemon			

1   Break open the Moreton Bay bug shells along the underside and lift out the meat. Cut across into slices about 2.5 cm/ 1 in thick.

2   Mix together the olive oil, wine, shallots and dill in a bowl. Add the lobster slices and stir to coat well. Cover and marinate for 30 minutes.

3   Mix together the mayonnaise, lemon rind and juice, lightly seasoning with salt and pepper. Spoon into a serving bowl and chill until needed.

4   Remove the lobster slices from the marinade and barbecue in a wire basket for about 5 minutes, or until cooked through, turning and basting once. Serve with the Lemon Mayonnaise.

 Preparation time: 20 minutes + 30 minutes marinating
Cooking time: 5 minutes

Butterflied Hot and Sour Prawns with Vietnamese Sauce

Serves 4

	METRIC	IMPERIAL	AMERICAN
Large raw prawns (jumbo shrimp)	450 g	1 lb	1 lb
Light soy sauce	45 ml	3 tbsp	3 tbsp
Clear honey	45 ml	3 tbsp	3 tbsp
Hoisin sauce	15 ml	1 tbsp	1 tbsp
Small red chilli, seeded and finely chopped	1	1	1
Garlic cloves, crushed	1	1	1
Piece of fresh root ginger, peeled and grated	2.5 cm	1 in	1 in
Caster (superfine) sugar	30 ml	2 tbsp	2 tbsp
Boiling water	30 ml	2 tbsp	2 tbsp
Juice of 1 lime			
Rice or sherry vinegar	45 ml	3 tbsp	3 tbsp
Nam pla (fish sauce)	45 ml	3 tbsp	3 tbsp

1   Shell and devein the prawns, leaving the tails on. Cut halfway through the back of each prawn, lengthways, then open out.

2   Mix the soy sauce, honey, hoisin sauce and chilli together in a bowl. Add the prawns and toss to coat. Cover and leave to marinate in the fridge for at least 1 hour.

3   Pound the garlic, ginger and sugar to a paste in a mortar with a pestle. Mix in the boiling water. Tip into a small serving bowl and stir in the remaining ingredients.

4   Barbecue the prawns for about 3 minutes on each side until pink and cooked through. Serve straight away with the Vietnamese Dipping Sauce.

Preparation time: 15 minutes + 1 hour marinating
Cooking time: 6 minutes

Roasted Lobster with Spiced Lime Baste

Serves 4

	METRIC	IMPERIAL	AMERICAN
Cooked lobsters, about 450 g/1 lb each	2	2	2
Sunflower oil	45 ml	3 tbsp	3 tbsp
Nam pla (fish sauce)	15 ml	1 tbsp	1 tbsp
Small red bird chilli, seeded and finely chopped	1	1	1
Lemon grass, finely chopped	5 ml	1 tsp	1 tsp
Finely grated lime rind	5 ml	1 tsp	1 tsp
Juice of 1 lime			
Chopped fresh coriander (cilantro)	15 ml	1 tbsp	1 tbsp
Caster (superfine) sugar	2.5 ml	½ tsp	½ tsp
Spring onions (scallions), thinly sliced on the diagonal	4	4	4

1 Lay the lobsters on a chopping board. Using a sharp, heavy knife, cut lengthways down the centre, through the head, body and tail. Remove and discard the inedible parts – the white round gravel sac near the head, the gills (which look like fingers) and the black intestinal vein.

2 Remove the claws and crack them open. Prise out the meat and put in the empty head shell. Gently loosen the meat in the lobster shells with a knife.

3 Put the oil, nam pla, chilli, lemon grass, lime rind and juice, coriander and sugar in a small jug and whisk together with a fork. Drizzle over the lobster meat.

4 Barbecue the lobster, shell-side down, for about 7 minutes, or until the lobster is hot. Scatter with spring onions and serve straight away.

Preparation time: 20 minutes
Cooking time: 7 minutes

Thai Coconut Crab

Seafood and chicken are often combined in Thai cuisine. The presentation of this recipe is a little unusual, however, as the ingredients are cooked in cleaned crab shells. Ask your fishmonger if you do not have any. Boil for 10 minutes to sterilise before use.

Serves 4

	METRIC	IMPERIAL	AMERICAN
Creamed coconut, finely chopped	25 g	1 oz	2 tbsp
Boiling water	60 ml	4 tbsp	4 tbsp
Skinless chicken breast	175 g	6 oz	6 oz
White crab meat	350 g	12 oz	12 oz
Garlic clove, crushed	1	1	1
Red chilli, seeded and finely chopped	1	1	1
Chopped fresh coriander (cilantro)	30 ml	2 tbsp	2 tbsp
Salt and freshly ground black pepper			
Sunflower oil	15 ml	1 tbsp	1 tbsp
Green Papaya and Carrot Salad (see page 123), to serve			

1   Put the creamed coconut in a bowl and pour over the boiling water. Mix to a smooth paste and leave to cool.

2   Chop the chicken breast very finely. Add to the coconut with the crab meat, garlic, chilli and coriander and season with salt and pepper. Mix together thoroughly.

3   Lightly brush the insides of four cleaned crab shells with oil, then spoon in the filling, dividing it equally between the shells.

4   Barbecue, filling-side up, for about 15 minutes, or until lightly set and cooked through. Serve hot with Green Papaya and Carrot Salad.

Preparation time: 15 minutes
Cooking time: 15 minutes

VEGETABLES, SALADS AND VEGETARIAN DISHES

Contrary to popular belief, barbecues don't have to be meaty affairs. There's a huge variety of vegetables that taste wonderful roasted over coals. Most need little preparation other than a simple brushing with flavoured oil or marinade to keep them succulent. Others, like corn on the cob and shallots, benefit from simmering first until almost tender.

Although vegetarianism is less common in Australia than in many parts of the world, the numerous fresh fruit and vegetables grown there make it simple to provide for those who prefer to avoid meat. You'll find a range of delicious recipes in this chapter which can be enjoyed by both vegetarians and meat-eaters alike.

Chargrilled Aubergines

Serves 4

	METRIC	IMPERIAL	AMERICAN
Small aubergines	2	2	2
Salt and freshly ground black pepper			
Garlic clove, crushed	1	1	1
Chopped fresh rosemary	15 ml	1 tbsp	1 tbsp
Finely grated rind and juice of 1 lemon			
Olive oil	60 ml	4 tbsp	4 tbsp

1 Cut the aubergines in half lengthways. Score the cut side in a criss-cross fashion, then sprinkle generously with salt. Leave for 15 minutes.

2 Meanwhile, mix together the garlic, rosemary, lemon rind and a little pepper.

3 Rinse the aubergines under cold water and pat dry on kitchen paper (paper towels). Brush the olive oil over the scored side of the aubergines and barbecue, scored side down, for about 8 minutes or until well browned. Turn over and scatter the garlic and rosemary mixture over the tops.

4 Cook for a further 6–7 minutes or until the aubergines are very tender. Sprinkle with lemon juice before serving.

 Preparation time: 20 minutes
Cooking time: 15 minutes

Fire-baked Jackets

Jacket potatoes are delicious with just a knob of butter but they are even better served with the selection of toppings I have suggested here. Make the toppings in advance (they only take about 5 minutes) and keep them in the fridge until you are ready to serve.

Serves 4

	METRIC	IMPERIAL	AMERICAN
Large washed baking potatoes, about 275 g/10 oz each	4	4	4
Sunflower oil	30 ml	2 tbsp	2 tbsp
Fine sea salt	5 ml	1 tsp	1 tsp
Butter, to serve			

1 Prick the potatoes in several places with a skewer or fork to prevent them bursting. Brush the skins with oil, then sprinkle with sea salt.

2 Wrap each potato in a piece of foil and barbecue for 30 minutes, turning occasionally to ensure even cooking.

3 Remove the foil and barbecue for a further 30 minutes, turning now and then, until the skin is lightly browned and the middle feels soft when pierced with a skewer.

4 Cut a deep cross in each potato, and, using a clean tea towel (dish cloth), gently press in the sides. Add a knob of butter and one of the following toppings, if liked.

 Preparation time: 5 minutes
Cooking time: 1 hour

Chunky Avocado Topping: Mix 1 finely chopped small onion with the juice of 1 lime. Leave to stand for 5 minutes. Peel and halve 2 ripe avocados. Remove the stones (pits) and roughly chop the flesh. Add to the onion with 150 ml/¼ pt/⅔ cup soured (dairy sour) cream, a dash of Tabasco sauce, salt and pepper. Lightly mash together with a fork.

Garlic Mushroom Topping: Gently fry (sauté) 2 crushed garlic cloves and 4 sliced spring onions (scallions) in 25 g/1 oz/2 tbsp butter for 2 minutes. Stir in 225 g/8 oz quartered button mushrooms and gently cook for 4–5 minutes until tender. Season well.

Soured Cream and Sun-dried Tomato Topping: Mix together 150 ml/¼ pt/⅔ cup soured (dairy sour) cream, 8 sun-dried tomatoes in oil, drained and finely chopped, 15 ml/1 tbsp snipped chives, salt and pepper.

Chilli-glazed Corn Cobs

Serves 4

	METRIC	IMPERIAL	AMERICAN
Fresh corn cobs	*4*	*4*	*4*
Butter, softened	*100 g*	*4 oz*	*½ cup*
Green chilli, seeded and finely chopped	*1*	*1*	*1*
Red chilli, seeded and finely chopped	*1*	*1*	*1*
Salt and freshly ground black pepper			

1 Remove the husks and trim the corn cobs. Add to a pan of boiling water, cover and simmer for 15 minutes. Drain well.

2 Meanwhile, beat the butter and chopped chillis together, seasoning with salt and pepper.

3 Lightly brush the chilli butter over the corn cobs and barbecue for about 15 minutes, turning frequently, until tender. Serve hot, topped with any remaining butter.

Preparation time: 15 minutes
Cooking time: 15 minutes

Grilled Asparagus with Balsamic Vinegar and Herb Dressing

Serves 4

	METRIC	IMPERIAL	AMERICAN
Asparagus	700 g	1½ lb	1½ lb
Dijon mustard	5 ml	1 tsp	1 tsp
A pinch of caster (superfine) sugar			
Balsamic vinegar	30 ml	2 tbsp	2 tbsp
Salt and freshly ground black pepper			
Olive oil	120 ml	4 fl oz	½ cup
Chopped mixed fresh herbs, such as chervil and chives	30 ml	2 tbsp	2 tbsp

1 Trim the asparagus to equal lengths. Whisk the mustard, sugar, vinegar and seasoning together in a bowl. Gradually whisk in the olive oil until thickened.

2 Put the asparagus in a bowl. Pour over half of the dressing and toss to coat. Leave to marinate for 15 minutes.

3 Remove the asparagus from the dressing and barbecue for about 4 minutes on each side, until just tender.

4 Place the asparagus on a warmed serving dish. Stir the chopped herbs into the remaining dressing and drizzle over the asparagus. Serve straight away.

 Preparation time: 5 minutes + 15 minutes marinating
Cooking time: 8 minutes

Barbecued Mixed Vegetables

Serves 4

	METRIC	IMPERIAL	AMERICAN
Button onions	12	12	12
Medium aubergine (eggplant)	1	1	1
Medium courgettes (zucchini)	2	2	2
Button mushrooms	12	12	12
Small bay leaves	8	8	8
Olive oil	60 ml	4 tbsp	4 tbsp
Red wine vinegar	15 ml	1 tbsp	1 tbsp
Ground paprika	2.5 ml	½ tsp	½ tsp
Salt and freshly ground black pepper			

1 Put the onions in a small pan, cover with cold water and bring to the boil. Simmer for 2 minutes, then drain and, when cool enough to handle, peel off the skins.

2 Trim the aubergine and courgettes and cut into thick slices, then cut the aubergine slices into quarters. Thread on to four metal skewers with the onions, mushrooms and bay leaves.

3 Mix the oil, vinegar, paprika, salt and pepper together and brush over the vegetables. Leave for 15 minutes.

4 Barbecue the kebabs for about 10 minutes, turning several times, until evenly browned. Serve hot.

 Preparation time: 15 minutes + 15 minutes marinating
Cooking time: 10 minutes

Roasted Peppers with Feta Cheese

Serves 4

	METRIC	IMPERIAL	AMERICAN
Large red, green or yellow (bell) peppers	4	4	4
Olive oil	45 ml	3 tbsp	3 tbsp
Feta cheese, crumbled	100 g	4 oz	½ cup
Lemon juice	15 ml	1 tbsp	1 tbsp
Stoned (pitted) black olives, halved	25 g	1 oz	2 tbsp
Pine nuts, toasted	25 g	1 oz	1 oz
Chopped or torn fresh basil	45 ml	3 tbsp	3 tbsp
Freshly ground black pepper			

1 Cut the peppers in half and remove the seeds, then cut each half into three pieces. Brush generously with olive oil and place in a wire basket or thread on to skewers.

2 Barbecue the peppers for about 10 minutes, turning several times and brushing with more oil if necessary.

3 Transfer the roasted peppers to a bowl and scatter with Feta cheese while still hot. Toss together, then sprinkle with lemon juice. Add the olives, pine nuts, basil and black pepper. Mix well and serve warm or cold.

Preparation time: 10 minutes
Cooking time: 10 minutes

Pesto Baby Potatoes

Serves 4

	METRIC	IMPERIAL	AMERICAN
Baby potatoes, scrubbed	450 g	1 lb	1 lb
A large sprig of fresh mint			
Pesto sauce	45 ml	3 tbsp	3 tbsp
Freshly ground black pepper			

1   Boil the potatoes in lightly salted water with the sprig of mint for 5 minutes, until almost tender. Drain.

2   Return the potatoes to the pan and spoon over the pesto sauce. Gently turn the potatoes in the sauce to coat them.

3   Put the potatoes in a single layer on a large double sheet of foil, shiny side up. Sprinkle with pepper, then bring the corners of the foil together and seal the edges well.

4   Barbecue for about 20 minutes, or until cooked through. Open the parcel carefully and serve the potatoes hot.

 Preparation time: 10 minutes
Cooking time: 20 minutes

Creamy Coconut Rice

This rice dish is best made the day before to allow the flavours to mingle. It can also be served hot if preferred.

Serves 4

	METRIC	IMPERIAL	AMERICAN
Brown rice	175 g	6 oz	¾ cup
Sunflower oil	15 ml	1 tbsp	1 tbsp
Canned coconut milk	400 ml	14 fl oz	1¾ cups
Salt	2.5 ml	½ tsp	½ tsp
Sesame oil	10 ml	2 tsp	2 tsp
Lemon juice	10 ml	2 tsp	2 tsp
Piece of fresh root ginger, peeled and grated	2 cm	¾ in	¾ in
Chopped fresh mint	15 ml	1 tbsp	1 tbsp
Chopped fresh coriander (cilantro)	30 ml	2 tbsp	2 tbsp
Freshly ground black pepper			
Green chilli, seeded and finely chopped, to garnish	1	1	1

1 Measure the volume of rice in a jug. Heat the oil in a large heavy-based saucepan, add the rice and stir for 1 minute, until all the grains are coated.

2 Make up the volume of the coconut milk to double that of the rice with water. Add to the rice with the salt. Bring to the boil, stir once, then cover and simmer for about 30 minutes, or according to the packet instructions, until all the liquid is absorbed.

3 Stir in the sesame oil, lemon juice, ginger, chopped mint and coriander and black pepper. Leave to cool. Spoon the rice into a serving bowl and garnish with a sprinkling of green chilli. Cover and chill in the fridge until ready to serve.

Preparation time: 10 minutes
Cooking time: 30 minutes

Fire-roasted Shallots

Serves 4

	METRIC	IMPERIAL	AMERICAN
Small shallots	20	20	20
Olive oil	45 ml	3 tbsp	3 tbsp
Balsamic vinegar	10 ml	2 tsp	2 tsp
A pinch of caster (superfine) sugar			
Salt and freshly ground black pepper			

1 Put the shallots in a saucepan. Pour over enough boiling water to cover, then simmer for 2 minutes. Drain and, when cool enough to handle, peel off the skins.

2 Mix together the olive oil, vinegar and sugar. Add the warm onions and toss to coat in the mixture. Thread on to soaked skewers.

3 Barbecue the shallots for about 8 minutes, turning frequently, until lightly charred and tender. Sprinkle with salt and pepper before serving.

Preparation time: 15 minutes
Cooking time: 10 minutes

New Potato Salad

Serves 4

	METRIC	IMPERIAL	AMERICAN
Small new potatoes, scrubbed	450 g	1 lb	1 lb
Wholegrain mustard	5 ml	1 tsp	1 tsp
Olive oil	30 ml	2 tbsp	2 tbsp
Tarragon vinegar	15 ml	1 tbsp	1 tbsp
Salt and freshly ground black pepper			
Rashers (slices) of streaky bacon, rinded	100 g	4 oz	4 oz
Hard-boiled (hard-cooked) eggs, finely chopped	2	2	2
Soured (dairy sour) cream	150 ml	¼ pint	⅔ cup
Snipped fresh chives	45 ml	3 tbsp	3 tbsp

1 Cook the potatoes in lightly salted boiling water for about 12 minutes, or until just tender. Drain them well and put in a bowl.

2 Whisk together the mustard, oil, vinegar, salt and pepper. Spoon over the hot potatoes and toss to coat evenly. Leave to cool.

3 Meanwhile, grill (broil) the bacon rashers until crisp. Drain on kitchen paper (paper towels), then crumble over the potatoes. Cover the salad and chill in the fridge until needed.

4 Remove the salad from the fridge about 20 minutes before serving to allow it to come to room temperature. Mix together the soured cream and chives and drizzle over the potatoes, then serve.

 Preparation time: 20 minutes

Green Papaya and Carrot Salad

Serves 4

	METRIC	IMPERIAL	AMERICAN
Green slightly unripe papayas (pawpaws)	2	2	2
Salt	15 ml	1 tbsp	1 tbsp
Carrots, peeled	350 g	12 oz	12 oz
Red chilli, seeded and finely chopped	1	1	1
Nam pla (fish sauce)	15 ml	1 tbsp	1 tbsp
Caster (superfine) sugar	5 ml	1 tsp	1 tsp
Juice of 2 limes			
Small sprigs of coriander (cilantro), to garnish			

1 Halve and scoop out the seeds of the papayas. Peel off the skin, then slice thinly and cut into matchstick strips. Place in a sieve (strainer) and sprinkle with the salt. Leave for 15 minutes, then rinse under cold running water and drain.

2 Thinly slice the carrots, then cut into strips of a similar size to the papaya. Mix the chilli, nam pla, sugar and lime juice together in a bowl. Add the carrot and papaya strips and toss to coat.

3 Cover the salad and allow to stand for at least 30 minutes before serving. Garnish with a scattering of small sprigs of coriander.

 Preparation time: 25 minutes + 30 minutes standing

Sesame Noodle Salad

Serves 4

	METRIC	IMPERIAL	AMERICAN
Chinese egg noodles	225 g	8 oz	8 oz
Sunflower oil	15 ml	1 tbsp	1 tbsp
Sesame oil	15 ml	1 tbsp	1 tbsp
Garlic clove, crushed	1	1	1
Red (bell) pepper, seeded and cut into thin strips	1	1	1
Shiitake mushrooms, sliced	100 g	4 oz	4 oz
Mangetout (snow peas), trimmed and halved	100 g	4 oz	4 oz
Thai red or green curry paste	10 ml	2 tsp	2 tsp
Crunchy peanut butter	15 ml	1 tbsp	1 tbsp
Canned coconut milk	200 ml	7 fl oz	scant 1 cup
Light soy sauce	15 ml	1 tbsp	1 tbsp
Lime juice	15 ml	1 tbsp	1 tbsp
Toasted sesame seeds	30 ml	2 tbsp	2 tbsp

1   Soak or cook the noodles according to the packet instructions. Drain thoroughly.

2   Heat the oils in a large frying pan (skillet) and stir-fry the garlic, pepper, mushrooms and mangetout for 2–3 minutes until tender, but still crisp. Add to the noodles.

3   Add the curry paste, peanut butter and coconut milk to the pan and simmer gently for 5 minutes, stirring occasionally, until reduced and slightly thickened. Remove from the heat and stir in the soy sauce and lime juice. Leave to cool.

4   Spoon the coconut sauce over the noodles and vegetables and gently toss together. Serve sprinkled with toasted sesame seeds.

 Preparation time: 20 minutes

Pasta and Tamarillo Salad

Tamarillos are tropical fruit, oval in shape with a tart, tomato-like flavour. The skin is inedible, so remember to peel them before using.

Serves 4

	METRIC	IMPERIAL	AMERICAN
Ripe tamarillos	4	4	4
Garlic clove, crushed	1	1	1
Olive oil	75 ml	5 tbsp	5 tbsp
Red wine vinegar	15 ml	1 tbsp	1 tbsp
Salt and freshly ground black pepper			
Vegetable stock cube	1	1	1
Pasta shells	350 g	12 oz	12 oz
Goats' cheese, crumbled	150 g	5 oz	⅔ cup
Chopped fresh basil or chervil	45 ml	3 tbsp	3 tbsp
Sprigs of fresh basil or chervil, to garnish			

1 Peel the tamarillos and cut into 5 mm/¼ in dice. Put them into a bowl with the garlic, oil, vinegar, salt and pepper. Whisk together with a fork.

2 Meanwhile, dissolve the stock cube in a large pan of boiling water. Add the pasta and cook for 10 minutes, or until just tender. Drain well and tip into a bowl.

3 Pour the tamarillo dressing over the hot pasta and toss gently until the pasta is coated. Leave until cool.

4 Stir the crumbled cheese and chopped basil or chervil into the pasta. Cover and chill until needed. Remove 20 minutes before serving to allow the salad to come to room temperature. Garnish with sprigs of basil or chervil.

 Preparation time: 15 minutes

Fruity Rice Salad

The flavour of this salad improves if made the day before serving.

Serves 4

	METRIC	IMPERIAL	AMERICAN
Mixed dried fruit, such as apricots, peaches and mangoes	175 g	6 oz	1 cup
Orange juice	100 ml	3½ fl oz	scant ½ cup
Lemon grass stalk	1	1	1
Mixed long-grain and wild rice	225 g	8 oz	1 cup
Salt	5 ml	1 tsp	1 tsp
Sunflower oil	60 ml	4 tbsp	4 tbsp
Sesame oil	30 ml	2 tbsp	2 tbsp
Sherry vinegar	30 ml	2 tbsp	2 tbsp
Freshly ground black pepper			
Small pineapple	1	1	1
Spring onions (scallions)	6	6	6
Chopped fresh mint	30 ml	2 tbsp	2 tbsp

1 Finely chop the dried fruit and put in a bowl. Pour over the orange juice, stir to coat the fruit, then cover and leave to soak in the fridge for at least 4 hours, or overnight.

2 Bruise the lemon grass stalk and put in a saucepan with the rice and salt. Add 1 litre/1¾ pts/4¼ cups cold water. Bring to the boil, cover and simmer for 10 minutes or until tender. Drain well, discarding the lemon grass.

3 Whisk together the sunflower and sesame oils, sherry vinegar and pepper. Stir through the rice with the soaked fruit and juices. Leave until cool.

4 Slice the top and base from the pineapple, then cut away the skin in downward strips with a sharp knife. Cut out the woody 'eyes' in diagonal strips and slice the fruit. Remove the central core from each slice, then cut the pineapple rings into small chunks.

5 Trim the spring onions and thinly slice on the diagonal. Stir into the rice with the pineapple chunks. Chill until required. Stir in the chopped mint just before serving.

 Preparation time: 25 minutes + 4 hours soaking

Nutty Veggie Burgers

Serves 4

	METRIC	IMPERIAL	AMERICAN
Can of chick peas (garbanzos)	400 g	14 oz	1 large
Sunflower oil	30 ml	2 tbsp	2 tbsp
Macadamia nuts or skinned hazelnuts (filberts), roughly chopped	50 g	2 oz	½ cup
Spring onions (scallions), finely chopped	6	6	6
Small carrot, coarsely grated	1	1	1
Eating (dessert) apple, grated	1	1	1
Wholegrain mustard	15 ml	1 tbsp	1 tbsp
Tomato purée (paste)	15 ml	1 tbsp	1 tbsp
Chopped fresh parsley	30 ml	2 tbsp	2 tbsp
Salt and freshly ground black pepper			
Wholemeal burger buns	4	4	4
Salad leaves, mayonnaise tomato ketchup (catsup) and chutney, to serve			

1 Drain the chick peas in a sieve (strainer) and rinse under cold water. Drain again, then tip into a bowl and mash with a fork until fairly smooth.

2 Heat 15 ml/1 tbsp of the oil in a small frying pan (skillet) and gently cook the chopped nuts for about 3 minutes until golden. Stir in the spring onions and carrots and cook for a further 2 minutes, to soften slightly.

3 Add the nuts, spring onions, carrots, apple, mustard, tomato purée and parsley to the bowl. Season generously with salt and pepper, then mix together. Shape into four burgers. Chill in the fridge for 1 hour.

4 Brush the burgers with the remaining oil and barbecue for about 10 minutes, turning once, until the outside is golden brown and crisp.

5 Toast the burger buns lightly for a few minutes, then serve the burgers in the buns, topped with salad leaves and with a choice of mayonnaise, ketchup and chutney.

 Preparation time: 15 minutes + 1 hour chilling
Cooking time: 10 minutes

Crunchy Red Coleslaw

Serves 6

	METRIC	IMPERIAL	AMERICAN
Red cabbage	*225 g*	*8 oz*	*8 oz*
Red-skinned eating (dessert) apple	*1*	*1*	*1*
Orange juice	*30 ml*	*2 tbsp*	*2 tbsp*
Small red onion, peeled	*1*	*1*	*1*
Raw beetroot (red beet)	*225 g*	*8 oz*	*8 oz*
English mustard powder	*2.5 ml*	*¹/₂ tsp*	*¹/₂ tsp*
Clear honey	*15 ml*	*1 tbsp*	*1 tbsp*
White wine vinegar	*5 ml*	*1 tsp*	*1 tsp*
Ground paprika	*2.5 ml*	*¹/₂ tsp*	*¹/₂ tsp*
Salt and freshly ground black pepper			

1 Shred the cabbage very finely, discarding any tough stalks. Quarter, core and slice the apple, leaving the skin on. Toss in the orange juice.

2 Thinly slice the red onion. Peel the beetroot, then grate finely. Put the fruit and vegetables in a large bowl.

3 Blend the mustard and honey until smooth. Stir in the vinegar and paprika. Season with salt and pepper.

4 Pour the dressing over the salad and toss to coat. Cover and chill in the fridge for at least 1 hour before serving, to allow the flavours to mingle.

 Preparation time: 10 minutes + 1 hour marinating

Sun-dried Tomato and Mozzarella Pizza Pies

Serves 4

	METRIC	IMPERIAL	AMERICAN
Packet of pizza base or bread mix	250 g	9 oz	9 oz
Dried mixed herbs	2.5 ml	½ tsp	½ tsp
Lukewarm water	250 ml	8 fl oz	1 cup
Olive oil	30 ml	2 tbsp	2 tbsp
Sun-dried tomatoes in oil, chopped	6	6	6
Mozzarella cheese, sliced	175 g	6 oz	6 oz
Bel Paese cheese, sliced	50 g	2 oz	2 oz
Salt and freshly ground black pepper			
Mixed green salad, to serve			

1 Tip the pizza or bread mix and herbs into a large bowl. Stir in the water and oil, then knead on a lightly floured surface for 5 minutes until smooth and elastic.

2 Divide the dough into eight equal pieces. Roll four of the pieces into 15 cm/6 in rounds and place each on oiled foil on a baking (cookie) sheet. Keep the remaining pieces of dough covered to prevent drying out.

3 Divide the tomatoes between the rounds, leaving a 1 cm/½ in border. Arrange the cheeses on top. Season with a little salt and pepper. Brush the edges with water.

4 Roll the reserved dough pieces into 15 cm/6 in rounds. Place over the filled dough circles and press the edges firmly to seal. Cover loosely with oiled clingfilm (plastic wrap) and leave to rise in a warm place for 15 minutes.

5 Oil the barbecue rack well, then cook the pizza pies on the foil for about 3 minutes on each side until browned and cooked through. Serve hot with a mixed green salad.

 Preparation time: 20 minutes + 15 minutes rising
Cooking time: 6 minutes

Cheese and Onion Sausages

Serves 4

	METRIC	IMPERIAL	AMERICAN
Fresh white breadcrumbs	175 g	6 oz	3 cups
Hard cheese, such as Cheddar, grated	100 g	4 oz	1 cup
A pinch of English mustard powder			
Spring onions (scallions), finely sliced	4	4	4
Snipped fresh chives	30 ml	2 tbsp	2 tbsp
Freshly grated nutmeg	1.5 ml	¼ tsp	¼ tsp
Salt and freshly ground black pepper			
Whole egg, beaten	1	1	1
Egg, separated	1	1	1
Butter, melted	25 g	1 oz	2 tbsp
Plain (all-purpose) flour	45 ml	3 tbsp	3 tbsp
Sweet and Sour Barbecue Sauce (see page 133) and Fire-baked Jackets (see page 114), to serve			

1   Put the breadcrumbs, cheese, mustard powder, spring onions, chives and nutmeg in a bowl. Season with salt and pepper and mix together.

2   Whisk the whole egg, the separated egg yolk and the melted butter together. Add to the breadcrumbs and mix well. Divide into eight equal pieces and shape into sausages.

3   Lightly whisk the remaining egg white with a fork. Dip in the sausages, one at a time, then roll in the flour to coat. Chill for at least 1 hour, or until ready to cook.

4   Barbecue the sausages for 10 minutes, turning frequently, until golden brown all over. Serve with Sweet and Sour Barbecue Sauce and Fire-baked Jackets.

Preparation time: 15 minutes + 1 hour chilling
Cooking time: 10 minutes

ACCOMPANIMENTS

Sauces, chutneys, relishes, salsas and crusty breads add
the final touch to barbecue food and lift it out of the
ordinary into something special.

Most of these accompaniments can be made well in
advance. If space on the barbecue is limited, cook
breads in the oven instead. Wrap in foil and cook at
200°C/400°F/gas mark 6 for about
15 minutes, opening the foil for the last 5 minutes to
allow it to brown. It's a good idea to keep a kitchen
timer to hand, though, as it's easy to forget there's food
in the oven when you're busy barbecuing in the garden.

Sweet and Sour Barbecue Sauce

Serves 4–6

	METRIC	IMPERIAL	AMERICAN
Sunflower oil	30 ml	2 tbsp	2 tbsp
Garlic clove, crushed	1	1	1
Medium onion, finely chopped	1	1	1
Red wine vinegar	150 ml	¼ pint	⅔ cup
Finely grated rind and juice of 1 small orange			
Ground ginger	2.5 ml	½ tsp	½ tsp
Tomato purée (paste)	45 ml	3 tbsp	3 tbsp
Dark brown sugar	30 ml	2 tbsp	2 tbsp
Salt and freshly ground black pepper			

1 Heat the oil in a saucepan and gently fry (sauté) the garlic and onion for about 5 minutes until soft. Stir in all the remaining ingredients.

2 Bring to the boil. Turn down the heat, cover and simmer gently for 15 minutes, stirring occasionally. Serve hot or cold.

 Preparation time: 20 minutes

Hot Bread with Herb Butter

Serves 4–6

	METRIC	IMPERIAL	AMERICAN
Long French sticks	2	2	2
Butter, softened	225 g	8 oz	1 cup
Garlic cloves, crushed	3	3	3
Freshly chopped herbs	60 ml	4 tbsp	4 tbsp
Salt and freshly ground black pepper			

1 Cut the bread to within about 1 cm/½ in of the bottom crust, in slanting slices about 2.5 cm/1 in apart.

2 Mix together the butter, garlic and herbs, seasoning with salt and pepper. Spread the butter over both sides of the slices of bread.

3 Wrap the French sticks separately in strong kitchen foil. (If the bread is too long to fit on the barbecue, cut the sticks in half.)

4 Barbecue for about 5 minutes on each side, until the butter has melted and the bread is crisp. Open the foil and serve hot.

 Preparation time: 15 minutes
Cooking time: 10 minutes

For a change, try one of these differently flavoured butters.

Anchovy Butter: Finely chop a drained 50 g/2 oz can of anchovies. Beat with 225 g/8 oz/1 cup unsalted butter and a grinding of black pepper.

Sun-dried Tomato and Basil Butter: Mix 225 g/8 oz/1 cup butter, 2 crushed garlic cloves, 8 finely chopped sun-dried tomatoes in oil, 60 ml/4 tbsp chopped fresh basil, salt and black pepper.

Sage and Mustard Butter: Mix 225 g/8 oz/1 cup butter, 45 ml/ 3 tbsp chopped fresh sage, 30 ml/2 tbsp mild French mustard, salt and black pepper.

Feta Cheese and Chilli Damper

If you can't get buttermilk, use milk instead and stir in 5 ml/ 1 tsp of lemon juice half an hour before using.

Serves 4

	METRIC	IMPERIAL	AMERICAN
Self-raising (self-rising) flour	350 g	12 oz	3 cups
Salt	2.5 ml	½ tsp	½ tsp
Butter	25 g	1 oz	2 tbsp
Feta cheese, crumbled	150 g	5 oz	⅔ cup
Red chilli, seeded and finely chopped	1	1	1
Chopped fresh oregano	15 ml	1 tbsp	1 tbsp
Buttermilk	300 ml	½ pint	1¼ cups

1 Sift the flour and salt into a mixing bowl and rub in the butter until the mixture resembles fine breadcrumbs.

2 Stir in the the Feta cheese, chilli and oregano. Make a well in the middle, pour in the buttermilk and mix to a soft dough. Lightly knead on a floured surface for a few seconds, until smooth.

3 Shape into an 18 cm/7 in round and place on a large doubled piece of floured foil, shiny side up. Make a cross on the top about 1 cm/½ in deep with a knife. Wrap loosely in the foil, allowing the damper room to rise.

4 Put the damper directly on the hot coals and cook for 12 minutes. Remove and secure the foil tightly, then turn and cook the other side for 5–10 minutes or until golden brown and the base sounds hollow when tapped. Break into wedges and serve warm.

Preparation time: 15 minutes
Cooking time: 20 minutes

Herb-scented Ciabatta

Serves 4

	METRIC	IMPERIAL	AMERICAN
Garlic cloves, chopped	3	3	3
Salt and freshly ground black pepper			
Chopped fresh rosemary	30 ml	2 tbsp	2 tbsp
Chopped fresh thyme	15 ml	1 tbsp	1 tbsp
Olive oil	90 ml	6 tbsp	6 tbsp
Ciabatta	1	1	1

1   Put the garlic in a mortar with the salt and pepper and crush with a pestle to a paste. Add the rosemary and thyme and crush to bruise the leaves. Mix in the olive oil.

2   Slice the ciabatta in half, then cut into thick slices. Generously brush the herb and garlic oil over.

3   Barbecue the ciabatta slices for about 3 minutes on each side, or until crisp and golden, brushing with any remaining herb and garlic oil. Serve straight away.

Preparation time: 10 minutes
Cooking time: 6 minutes

Spicy Pineapple Chutney

Serves 8

	METRIC	IMPERIAL	AMERICAN
Medium pineapple, peeled, cored and diced	1	1	1
Granulated sugar	350 g	12 oz	1½ cups
Finely grated rind and juice of ½ lemon			
Sherry vinegar	60 ml	4 tbsp	4 tbsp
Ground cinnamon	5 ml	1 tsp	1 tsp
Ground ginger	2.5 ml	2.5 ml	2.5 ml
A pinch of ground turmeric			
Salt	2.5 ml	½ tsp	½ tsp

1 Put all ingredients in a large heavy-based saucepan. Heat gently until the sugar has dissolved.

2 Bring to the boil, turn down the heat and simmer for about 20 minutes or until thick and syrupy.

3 Spoon into hot, sterilised jars, cover and seal. Alternatively, allow to cool and serve.

Preparation time: 5 minutes
Cooking time: 25 minutes

Peach and Port Chutney

Serves 4

	METRIC	IMPERIAL	AMERICAN
Dried peaches, chopped	100 g	4 oz	²/₃ cup
Finely grated rind and juice of 1 orange			
Red onion, finely chopped	1	1	1
Dried red chilli, seeded and crushed	1	1	1
Caster (superfine) sugar	60 ml	4 tbsp	4 tbsp
Ruby port	150 ml	¼ pint	²/₃ cup
Chopped fresh coriander (cilantro)	45 ml	3 tbsp	3 tbsp
Salt and freshly ground black pepper			

1 Put the peaches, orange rind and juice, onion, chilli, sugar and port in a saucepan. Slowly bring to the boil. Cover and simmer for 5 minutes.

2 Remove the lid and simmer for a further 5 minutes, stirring occasionally, until thick and syrupy. Leave to cool.

3 Stir in the chopped coriander and season with a little salt and pepper. Spoon into a bowl to serve.

Preparation time: 10 minutes
Cooking time: 10 minutes

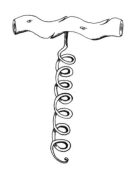

Fresh Mint and Apple Relish

Serves 4–6

	METRIC	IMPERIAL	AMERICAN
Eating (dessert) apples	3	3	3
Clear honey	30 ml	2 tbsp	2 tbsp
Cider vinegar	30 ml	2 tbsp	2 tbsp
Chopped fresh mint	30 ml	2 tbsp	2 tbsp
Ground allspice	1.5 ml	¼ tsp	¼ tsp
A pinch of salt			

1 Quarter, core and peel the apples. Put in a food processor with the honey and vinegar and process until finely chopped, but not puréed.

2 Tip into a serving bowl and stir in the mint, allspice and salt. Mix well and leave for 30 minutes before serving.

 Preparation time: 5 minutes + 30 minutes standing

Mango and Guava Relish

Serves 4

	METRIC	IMPERIAL	AMERICAN
Guavas, peeled and diced	2	2	2
Ripe mango, peeled and diced	1	1	1
Lemon juice	15 ml	1 tbsp	1 tbsp
Caster (superfine) sugar	15 ml	1 tbsp	1 tbsp
Red chilli, seeded and chopped	1	1	1

1 Toss the diced guava and mango with the lemon juice, sugar and chilli. Spoon into a serving bowl.

2 Cover and leave to marinate for at least 1 hour before serving, or overnight if preferred.

 Preparation time: 10 minutes + 1 hour marinating

Marinated Cucumber

Serves 4

	METRIC	IMPERIAL	AMERICAN
Cucumbers	2	2	2
Salt	50 g	2 oz	¼ cup
Caster (superfine) sugar	50 g	2 oz	¼ cup
Dry white wine	150 ml	¼ pint	⅔ cup
White wine vinegar	15 ml	1 tbsp	1 tbsp
Chopped fresh dill (dill weed)	60 ml	4 tbsp	4 tbsp
Freshly ground black pepper			

1 Thinly slice the cucumbers and place in a colander, sprinkling salt between the layers. Put the colander in the sink or over a bowl and leave to drain for 1 hour.

2 Thoroughly rinse the cucumber under cold running water to remove the salt. Pat dry on kitchen paper (paper towels).

3 Put the sugar and wine in a saucepan and heat gently until the sugar has dissolved. Remove from the heat and leave to cool. Stir in the vinegar, then add the cucumber slices, cover and marinate for 1 hour.

4 Drain the cucumber and tip into a bowl. Add the dill and a little black pepper and mix well. Chill in the fridge until ready to serve.

 Preparation time: 10 minutes + 2 hours draining and marinating

DESSERTS AND DRINKS

Here you'll find a selection of delicious desserts to round off your barbecue. Many can be cooked over the cooling coals while you eat your main course. Fruit's a popular choice and is perfect for a light finish to the meal. Others, like pavlova, the classic Australian dessert, can be prepared in advance and kept in the fridge until ready to serve.

Ice cream makes an excellent standby, either to serve with barbecued fruit, or to eat on its own if you haven't had time to make a dessert.

Long refreshing drinks are a must in hot weather. Cool off with ice-cold lager and a choice of soft drinks. Australia produces some wonderful rich wines – a chilled Chardonnay is an excellent white to serve at a barbecue or choose a spicy red such as Cabernet Sauvignon, Shiraz, or Coonawarra claret. Alternatively, try one of our thirst-quenching punches; sit back in your deckchair with a Sydney Sunset and watch the coals glow as the sun goes down!

Singed Bananas with Brazil Nut Butter

Serves 4

	METRIC	IMPERIAL	AMERICAN
Bananas, unpeeled	4	4	4
Unsalted butter, softened	40 g	1½ oz	3 tbsp
Soft light brown sugar	25 g	1 oz	1 oz
Brazil nuts, chopped and toasted	50 g	2 oz	2 oz
Lemon juice	5 ml	1 tsp	1 tsp
Ground cinnamon	1.5 ml	¼ tsp	¼ tsp
A pinch of ground ginger			
Vanilla or toffee ice cream, to serve			

1   Lay the bananas on the barbecue and cook for about 15 minutes, turning once, until the skins are completely blackened.

2   Cream the butter and sugar together, then mix in the nuts, lemon juice, cinnamon and ginger.

3   Split the banana skins along one edge and carefully open. Spoon the Brazil Nut Butter into the split and allow to melt. Serve each with a scoop of ice cream. Eat out of the skins with a spoon.

Preparation time: 5 minutes
Cooking time: 15 minutes

Barbecued Toffee Apples

Check the apples towards the end of cooking time and remove from the heat as soon as they are ready, as they'll collapse if overcooked.

Serves 4

	METRIC	IMPERIAL	AMERICAN
Cooking (tart) apples	4	4	4
Butter, softened	50 g	2 oz	¼ cup
Light soft brown sugar	50 g	2 oz	¼ cup
Golden (light corn) syrup	15 ml	1 tbsp	1 tbsp
Ground almonds	25 g	1 oz	¼ cup
Macadamia nuts, toasted and roughly chopped	50 g	2 oz	½ cup
Stem ginger, finely chopped	25 g	1 oz	2 tbsp
Whipped cream or ice cream, to serve			

1 Core the apples and score around the middle of each to prevent the skins from splitting during cooking.

2 Mix together the remaining ingredients, then spoon into the apple cavities. Place each apple on a square of double-thickness foil, then bring the corners together to make a parcel and enclose the apple.

3 Barbecue for about 25 minutes or until the apples are very tender. Unwrap the parcels and serve the apples with whipped cream or ice cream.

 Preparation time: 10 minutes
Cooking time: 25 minutes

Hot Pear and White Chocolate Crunch

Serves 4

	METRIC	IMPERIAL	AMERICAN
Firm pears	4	4	4
Butter, melted	15 g	½ oz	1 tbsp
Orange or almond liqueur	15 ml	1 tbsp	1 tbsp
Orange or lemon juice	10 ml	2 tsp	2 tsp
Amaretti biscuits (cookies)	4	4	4
Clear honey	15 ml	1 tbsp	1 tbsp
White chocolate, chopped	50 g	2 oz	2 oz
Crème fraîche or Mascarpone cheese, to serve			

1   Cut the pears in half lengthwise. Using a teaspoon or melon baller, scoop out the core and discard.

2   Mix together the butter, liqueur and orange or lemon juice. Reserve 15 ml/1 tbsp, then brush the remainder over the cut surfaces of the pears.

3   Roughly crush the biscuits and mix with the reserved butter glaze, the honey and white chocolate. Divide the mixture between the pears, spooning it into mounds where the cores have been removed.

4   Put the pears on to squares of double-thickness foil, laying two halves side by side on each, then bring the corners together to make a parcel, completely enclosing the pears.

5   Barbecue the parcels for about 15 minutes or until the pears are tender and the filling warm and melted. Serve with crème fraîche or Mascarpone cheese.

Preparation time: 15 minutes
Cooking time: 15 minutes

Scorched Pineapple with Brandy Butterscotch Sauce

Serves 4

	METRIC	IMPERIAL	AMERICAN
Large ripe pineapple	1	1	1
Clear honey	30 ml	2 tbsp	2 tbsp
Unsalted butter	50 g	2 oz	¼ cup
Demerara sugar	175 g	6 oz	¾ cup
Double (heavy) cream	300 ml	½ pint	1¼ cups
Brandy	30 ml	2 tbsp	2 tbsp

1 Top and tail the pineapple. Cut away the skin, then cut out the hard 'eyes'. Slice the fruit into eight wedges and cut away the central core from each piece. Brush with the honey.

2 Put the butter and sugar in a heavy-based pan and heat until the sugar has completely dissolved, stirring frequently. (This takes about 10 minutes.) Remove from the heat and cool for 3 minutes.

3 Stir in the cream and brandy, then return to the heat and simmer for 2 minutes, stirring until smooth. Set aside until needed.

4 Barbecue the pineapple wedges for about 3 minutes on each side until lightly scorched. Serve hot with the Brandy Butterscotch Sauce poured over.

Preparation time: 15 minutes
Cooking time: 6 minutes

Tropical Fruit Feast with Passion Fruit Cream

Serves 4–6

	METRIC	IMPERIAL	AMERICAN
Small pineapple	1	1	1
Small mango	1	1	1
Sharon fruit	2	2	2
Bananas	2	2	2
White rum or orange-flavoured liqueur	60 ml	4 tbsp	4 tbsp
Unsalted butter, melted	15 g	½ oz	1 tbsp
Caster (superfine) sugar	50 g	2 oz	¼ cup
Double (heavy) cream	300 ml	½ pint	1¼ cups
Passion fruit, pulp only	3	3	3

1   Peel the pineapple and remove the woody 'eyes'. Cut into thick slices, remove the central core with an apple corer and cut each slice into four pieces.

2   Peel and cut the mango into large chunks, discarding the stone (pit). Peel and thickly slice the sharon fruit and bananas. Cut the sharon fruit slices in half.

3   Put the fruit in a large bowl. Mix together 30 ml/2 tbsp of the rum or liqueur, the melted butter and half the sugar. Spoon over the fruit and toss well to coat. Thread the fruit on to soaked wooden skewers.

4   Whip the cream into soft peaks. Gently fold in the passion fruit pulp, the remaining rum or liqueur and the sugar. Spoon into a serving bowl and chill until needed.

5   Barbecue the fruit kebabs for about 5 minutes, turning once, until slightly caramelised. Serve hot with the chilled Passion Fruit Cream.

 Preparation time: 20 minutes
Cooking time: 5 minutes

Watermelon Sorbet

Serves 4

	METRIC	IMPERIAL	AMERICAN
Piece of watermelon	*900 g*	*2 lb*	*2 lb*
Lime or lemon juice	*30 ml*	*2 tbsp*	*2 tbsp*
Caster (superfine) sugar	*100 g*	*4 oz*	*½ cup*
Cranberry juice	*100 ml*	*3½ fl oz*	*scant ½ cup*
Sprigs of fresh mint, to decorate			

1 Scoop the flesh out of the watermelon, discarding the seeds. Put in a food processor with the lime or lemon juice and blend until smooth.

2 Put the sugar and cranberry juice in a small pan and heat gently until dissolved. Leave to cool.

3 Stir the sugar syrup into the melon purée and pour into a freezerproof container. Freeze for 3 hours or until half-frozen. Return to the freezer for a further 30 minutes, then whisk again. Repeat the freezing and whisking once more, then freeze until solid.

4 Scoop into balls on to a tray and return to the freezer until required. Serve in chilled glasses or bowls and garnish with sprigs of fresh mint.

 Preparation time: 15 minutes + freezing

Mocha and Macademia Truffle Cake

Macademia trees grow in the woodlands of Australia and produce round white nuts, also known as Queensland nuts, with a crisp texture and buttery flavour.

Serves 6–8

	METRIC	IMPERIAL	AMERICAN
Unsalted macadamia nuts	100 g	4 oz	1 cup
Butter, diced	100 g	4 oz	½ cup
Caster (superfine) sugar	100 g	4 oz	½ cup
Very strong cold black coffee	60 ml	4 tbsp	4 tbsp
Plain (semi-sweet) chocolate	250 g	9 oz	9 oz
Eggs, separated	4	4	4
Icing (confectioners') sugar, to decorate			

1 Put the macadamia nuts on a baking (cookie) tray and roast in a preheated oven at 160°C/325°F/gas mark 3 for 5–8 minutes or until light golden. Leave to cool, then put in a food processor and finely grind.

2 Put the butter, sugar, coffee and chocolate in a bowl over a pan of simmering water. Stir occasionally until melted, then remove from the heat and cool for 5 minutes. Stir in the ground macadamia nuts and egg yolks.

3 Whisk the egg whites until soft peaks form. Stir one-third into the chocolate mixture, then gently fold in the rest. Spoon into a greased and base-lined 20 cm/8 in springclip tin (pan).

4 Bake the truffle cake for 1 hour or until firm. Leave to cool in the tin, then remove and peel off the lining paper. Dust with icing sugar before serving.

Preparation time: 25 minutes
Cooking time: 1 hour

Roasted Rum and Raisin Peaches

Serves 4

	METRIC	IMPERIAL	AMERICAN
Raisins	25 g	1 oz	⅙ cup
Rum	30 ml	2 tbsp	2 tbsp
Mascarpone or cream cheese	50 g	2 oz	¼ cup
Firm peaches	4	4	4
Butter, melted	25 g	1 oz	2 tbsp
Caster (superfine) sugar	15 ml	1 tbsp	1 tbsp

1   Put the raisins in a small bowl. Spoon over the rum, cover
and leave to soak for at least 2 hours, or overnight. Beat the
Mascarpone or cream cheese until soft, then mix in the
rum-soaked raisins.

2   Cut the peaches in half and remove the stones (pits). Brush
the cut sides generously with melted butter, then sprinkle
with the sugar.

3   Barbecue for about 3 minutes on each side until lightly
browned and softened. Fill each with a spoonful of the
raisin and Mascarpone mixture and serve as soon as it
begins to melt.

Preparation time: 10 minutes + 2 hours soaking
Cooking time: 6 minutes

Peach Melba Mousse with Kiwi Coulis

Serves 4

	METRIC	IMPERIAL	AMERICAN
Ginger biscuits (cookies)	175 g	6 oz	6 oz
Butter, melted	50 g	2 oz	¼ cup
Marshmallows	200 g	7 oz	7 oz
Can of peaches, drained	400 g	14 oz	1 large
Double (heavy) cream	300 ml	½ pint	1¼ cups
Ripe kiwi fruit	3	3	3
Icing (confectioners') sugar, sifted	25 g	1 oz	⅙ cup

1 Grease and line the base of a 20 cm/8 in springclip tin (pan). Crush the ginger biscuits and mix with the melted butter. Spoon into the tin and press down well with the back of a spoon. Chill in the fridge while making the filling.

2 Put the marshmallows in a non-stick pan and heat gently for about 3 minutes, until melted. Leave to cool. Meanwhile, finely chop the peaches. Lightly whip the cream until soft peaks form.

3 Fold the melted marshmallows and peaches into the cream. Spoon over the ginger base in the tin, smoothing the top with the back of a spoon. Chill in the fridge for at least 2 hours.

4 Meanwhile, peel the kiwi fruit, roughly chop and put in a food processor. Blend until smooth. Add the icing sugar and blend again. Pour into a jug and chill until needed.

5 Remove the mousse from the tin and place on a serving plate. Serve cut into wedges with a little of the Kiwi Coulis poured over.

 Preparation time: 20 minutes + 2 hours chilling

Pineapple Sundowner

This makes a delicious non-alcoholic cooler if you leave out the rum.

Serves 6–8

	METRIC	IMPERIAL	AMERICAN
Caster (superfine) sugar	175 g	6 oz	¾ cup
Star anise	2	2	2
Cold water	300 ml	½ pint	1¼ cups
Medium pineapple	1	1	1
Juice of 2 lemons			
White rum	100 ml	3½ fl oz	scant ½ cup

Crushed ice and chilled sparkling mineral, soda water or ginger ale, to serve

1 Put the sugar, star anise and water in a saucepan and heat gently until the sugar dissolves. Bring to the boil and simmer for 2 minutes. Remove from the heat and leave to cool.

2 Peel and quarter the pineapple. Remove the woody central core, then chop the pineapple into chunks. Put in a food processor with the lemon juice and blend to a purée.

3 Mix the pineapple purée and sugar syrup together, then strain into a jug. Stir in the rum. Cover and chill in the fridge until ready to serve.

4 Pour over crushed iced in tall glasses and serve topped with mineral or soda water or ginger ale, to taste.

 Preparation time: 15 minutes

Exotic Fruit Pavlova

This meringue with its crisp outside and marshmallow middle was named after the ballerina Anna Pavlova, when she toured Australia in the 1930s. It's a traditional barbecue dessert, often brought along by the guests.

Serves 6–8

	METRIC	IMPERIAL	AMERICAN
Egg whites	3	3	3
Cream of tartar	2.5 ml	½ tsp	½ tsp
Caster (superfine) sugar	175 g	6 oz	¾ cup
Cornflour (cornstarch), sifted	5 ml	1 tsp	1 tsp
White wine vinegar	5 ml	1 tsp	1 tsp
Double (heavy) cream	150 ml	¼ pint	⅔ cup
Orange flower or rose water	5 ml	1 tsp	1 tsp
Crème fraîche	150 ml	¼ pint	⅔ cup
Exotic fruits such as mango, papaya, guava and kiwi, sliced	450 g	1 lb	1 lb
Icing (confectioners') sugar	15 ml	1 tbsp	1 tbsp

1 Preheat the oven to 140°C/275°F/gas mark 1. Draw a 20 cm/8 in circle on non-stick baking parchment and place on a baking (cookie) sheet.

2 Whisk the egg whites with the cream of tartar until stiff, but not dry. Gradually whisk in the sugar 15 ml/1 tbsp at a time until the meringue is stiff and shiny. Blend the cornflour and vinegar together, then quickly whisk into the mixture.

3 Spoon the meringue on to the baking sheet, spreading out to the diameter of the marked circle. Make a slight hollow in the middle.

4 Bake for 1 hour, then turn off the heat and leave to cool in the oven (this helps to prevent the meringue cracking). Peel the lining paper off the meringue. Place on a serving plate.

5 Whip the cream with the orange flower or rose water until soft peaks form. Fold in the crème fraîche. Spoon over the meringue. Arrange the fruits on top of the cream. Dust with icing sugar before serving.

 Preparation time: 10 minutes + cooling
Cooking time: 1 hour

Spiced Iced Lemon Tea

Serves 6–8

	METRIC	IMPERIAL	AMERICAN
Water	900 ml	1½ pints	3¾ cups
Lemon tea bags	3	3	3
Cinnamon stick	1	1	1
Clove	1	1	1
Demerara sugar	30 ml	2 tbsp	2 tbsp
Ice cubes, lemon slices and sprigs of mint, to serve			

1 Bring the water to the boil in a saucepan. Add the tea bags, cinnamon stick, clove and sugar. Leave for a minute, then stir to dissolve the sugar. Cover and leave to infuse for 4 more minutes.

2 Strain the tea into a heatproof jug, discarding the tea bags but not the spices. Leave to cool, then chill in the fridge for at least 4 hours. Remove the spices, then serve with plenty of ice and decorate with slices of lemon and sprigs of mint.

 Preparation time: 10 minutes + 4 hours chilling

Honeyed Figs with Coconut Ice Cream

Bring out the fragrant flavour of ripe figs by cooking them over the cooling embers of the barbecue.

Serves 4

	METRIC	IMPERIAL	AMERICAN
Can of coconut milk	400 ml	14 fl oz	1 large
Egg yolks	4	4	4
Caster (superfine) sugar	75 g	3 oz	1/3 cup
Double (heavy) cream	200 ml	7 fl oz	scant 1 cup
Clear honey	60 ml	4 tbsp	4 tbsp
White wine	30 ml	2 tbsp	2 tbsp
Ripe figs	12	12	12

1   Pour the coconut milk into a non-stick saucepan and bring to the boil. Whisk the egg yolks and sugar together until thick, then pour over the boiling coconut milk.

2   Return the mixture to the pan and cook, stirring, over a very gentle heat until slightly thickened, taking care not to let the mixture boil.

3   Leave to cool, stirring occasionally. Stir in the cream, then pour into a shallow freezerproof container and freeze for 2 hours. Whisk the mixture to break up the ice crystals, then freeze for a further hour.

4   Repeat the whisking and freezing once more. Finally, return the ice cream to the freezer for at least 4 hours, or overnight.

5   Gently heat the honey and wine in a small pan until warm. Halve the figs and dip into the mixture.

6 Barbecue the figs for 2–3 minutes on each side, brushing frequently with the honey mixture. Serve hot with scoops of coconut ice cream.

 Preparation time: 35 minutes + freezing
Cooking time: 6 minutes

Sydney Sunset

Serves 6–8

	METRIC	IMPERIAL	AMERICAN
1 lime			
Caster (superfine) sugar	50 g	2 oz	¼ cup
Piece of fresh root ginger, peeled and thinly sliced	5 cm	2 in	2 in
Cranberry juice	600 ml	1 pint	2½ cups
75 cl bottle fruity white wine, chilled	1	1	1
Ice and chilled sparkling mineral or soda water, to serve			

1 Pare the rind off the lime and place in a saucepan with the sugar, ginger and cranberry juice. Heat gently, stirring occasionally until the sugar dissolves. Bring to the boil and simmer for 5 minutes. Cover and leave to cool.

2 Strain the syrup into a serving jug. Squeeze the lime juice and stir in with the wine. Cover and chill in the fridge for at least 3 hours, or until ready to serve.

3 Pour into tall glasses and serve with plenty of ice and sparkling mineral or soda water if liked.

 Preparation time: 15 minutes + 3 hours chilling

INDEX

Other Foulsham titles

ISBN: 0-572-02417-7

ISBN: 0-572-02418-5

ISBN: 0-572-02508-4

Available from all good bookshops